Spain

160 km / 100 miles

Atlantic

Ocean

FRANCE

Nîmes
Montpellier
Sète
Perpignan
C. Creus
Toulouse
Carcassonne
Girona
PYRENEES
Pau
Tarbes
ANDORRA
Barcelona
Bayonne
Terrassa
San Sebastián
Pamplona
Lérida
Tarragona
Bilbao
Logroño
Zaragoza
Ebro
CANTÁBRICA
Santander
Soria
Calatayud
Tortosa
Castellón de la Plana
Gijón
Burgos
Duero
Teruel
C. de la Nao
Oviedo
CORDILLERA
Valladolid
Segovia
Valencia
León
ESPAÑA
(SPAIN)
Alcalá de Henares
Júcar
Alicante
Elx
Bellavente
Cuenca
C. Ortegal
El Ferrol
Salamanca
Madrid
Albacete
Cartagena
La Coruña
Toledo
Murcia
C. Finisterre
Tajo
Ciudad Real
Aguilas
Lugo
Guadiana
Valdepeñas
C. de Gata
Orense
Guarda
Cáceres
Almadén
Jaén
Almería
Vigo
Braga
Castelo Branco
SIERRA MORENA
Guadalquivir
SIERRA
NEVADA
Melilla (Sp.)
Douro
Zafra
Córdoba
Granada
Porto
Aveiro
Badajoz
Málaga
Costa del Sol
Coimbra
Leiria
Santarém
Évora
Seville
Marbella
Gibraltar (Sp.)
PORTUGAL
Beja
Jerez de la Frontera
Ceuta (Sp.)
Tétouan
Lisbon
Huelva
Cádiz
Tarifa
Tanger
MOROCCO
Setúbal
Faro
Lagos
C. de S. Vicente
Larache

Mediterranean

Sea

MENORCA
ISLAS BALEARES
(BALEARIC ISLANDS)
MALLORCA
Palma
FORMENTERA
IBIZA

ALGERIA
Algier
Blida
Chott El Hodna
Ech Cheliff
Mostaganem
Oran
Tlemcen

**ISLAS CANARIAS (SP).
(CANARY ISLANDS)**

LA PALMA
TENERIFE
Sta. Cruz de Tenerife
LANZAROTE
FUERTEVENTURA
GOMERA
GRAN CANARIA
Las Palmas
HIERRO

BIENVENIDO

This is a guidebook that takes you straight to the heart of three famous Spanish cities: Seville, Córdoba and Granada. These are the crown jewels of southern Spain, a compact trinity of historic capitals which embraces a prodigious wealth of monuments and sights, several of which get into the 'wonders of the world' class. This trinity of cities is also vibrant with all the exuberance of the new, confident Spain – a winning combination of ancient and modern that is making Andalusia one of the most fulfilling places that you can visit in Europe.

Insight Pocket Guide: Seville, Córdoba and Granada is a straightforward, feet-friendly guide to exploring and enjoying these three great cities. Like a good friend, the author Nigel Tisdall takes you on detailed day-long and half-day walks that show you the best of each city. Thus, the itineraries cover the famous attractions, inviting you to explore Seville's massive cathedral and climb the mighty Giralda, wander inside the great Mezquita or mosque of Córdoba and picnic in the gardens of the Alhambra in Granada; they also take you down the back streets and beyond the clichés, into the old Jewish and Moorish quarters, with frequent recommendations for shopping, lunch and *tapas* en route.

Within this book Nigel Tisdall also provides a guide to Expo '92, the six-month-long fiesta that has revitalised Seville as it plays host to the world's celebrations for the 500th anniversary of Columbus's discovery of America. He includes an insight into the region's history, along with a calendar of Andalusia's busy programme of fiestas, fairs and religious celebrations. He also offers advice on where to find the best restaurants, hotels and markets, and how to attend and fully appreciate the Andalusian arts of bullfighting and flamenco.

Whether you're taking a short break in one of the three cities in this book and need to know exactly where to go, or spending a week or fortnight visiting all three, Nigel Tisdall, who is also the author of Insight Pocket Guides to Tenerife and Brittany, is the perfect companion for your trip. Follow his suggestions for the best of Spain.

Bienvenido! Welcome!

Insight Pocket Guide:
Seville, Córdoba & Granada

First Edition

© **1992 APA Publications (HK) Ltd**

All Rights Reserved

Printed in Singapore by:
Höfer Press (Pte) Ltd, Singapore

INSIGHT *Pocket* GUIDES

Sevilla
CORDOBA & GRANADA

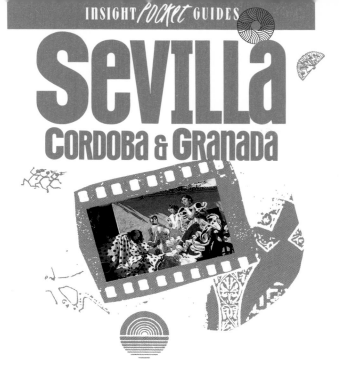

Author **Nigel Tisdall**
Photographers **Nigel Tisdall** *and* **Lyle Lawson**

INSIGHT
Pocket
GUIDES

Contents

Welcome...1
Dear Reader...8
History and Culture

Roman and Moorish Andalusia...............**10**

The Reconquest......................................**12**

Travellers and Romantics.......................**14**

Columbus Was Everywhere....................**15**

Architectural Terms...............................**16**

Historical Outline....................................**17**

Seville..**19**

1. Cathedral and Parque de María Luisa.....**20**

2. La Maestranza and Reales Alcázares.......**25**

3. City Walk via Casa de Pilatos................**30**

4. Museums..**33**

Expo '92..**35**

Highlights..**38**

Entertainment..**39**

Getting There..**41**

Tickets and Information..............................**41**

Calendar of Events....................................**42**

Córdoba...**44**

5. La Mezquita: A Guided Tour..................**45**

A Forest of Marble Palms.......................**46**

6. Exploring the Judería............................**50**

7. City Walk and Museums........................**51**

Granada...**54**

8. Alhambra I: Alcazaba and Generalife.......**55**

The Tale of the Alhambra.......................**57**

Visiting the Alhambra.............................**58**

9. Alhambra II: Nasrid Palaces and
    Gardens..**59**

10. Exploring the Albaicín.........................**62**

11. Morning Walk in the Cathedral
Quarter **64**

Shopping **66**

Eating Out **70**

Entertainment **74**

Calendar of Special Events **78**

Practical Information

Travel Essentials **82**

When to Go **82**

Climate **82**

Time Difference **82**

Documents **83**

Money Matters **83**

Health **83**

Clothing **83**

Electricity **83**

Photography **83**

On Departure **83**

Getting There **83**

By Air **83**

Package Deals **84**

By Rail **84**

By Road **84**

Getting Around **84**

Maps and Guides **84**

By Car **84**

Car Hire **84**

By Train **85**

By Coach and Bus **85**

By Taxi **85**

Accommodation **85**

Hotels **85**

Seville **86**

Córdoba...86
Granada..86
Camping..87
Useful Information........................87
Tourist Offices................................87
Tipping and Service.......................87
Facilities for the Disabled..............87
Children..87
Duty Free..88
Consulates in Seville.....................88
Media & Communication..............88
Telephone.......................................88
Business Hours.............................89
Health & Emergencies..................89
Emergencies...................................89
Police..90
Toilets...90
Further Reading............................90
Index...92

Maps

Spain...IFC
Seville...18
Seville Cathedral..........................20
Seville: Reales Alcázares............25
Expo '92..34
Córdoba..44
La Mezquita..................................47
Granada...54
Alhambra I: Alcazaba and Generalife...................................56
Alhambra II: Nasrid Palaces and Gardens.....................................59
Andalusia......................................96

Dear Reader

My first visit to Andalusia was by train, travelling south from Madrid in an old stiff-backed compartment decorated with lace curtains, table lamps and framed black-and-white photos of since-developed resorts. The carriages bulged with life: conscripted youth, families off to weddings, beggars heading south for the winter, gift-laden Moroccans returning home. Cramped four-a-side in a fog of smoke, strangers nattered and laughed amidst a rising tide of breadcrumbs and sunflower seeds as the sun dropped behind terracotta hills freckled with olives, vines and cork oaks.

On a recent trip to Andalusia I again took the train – this time a *Talgo*, one of the sleek pencil-like expresses that now glide around the New Spain. Sitting in my computer-selected seat, confronted by ranks of video screens, compulsory canned music and blinds pulled low to obscure the now *outré* landscape, I was surrounded by chic Spaniards poring over TV magazines and earplugging into football. I felt like asking the conductor if it was now a criminal offence to board the train wearing a beret or carrying a scythe.

Progress is always a mixed blessing – of course I now had air-conditioned comfort and a shorter journey time, but I had little desire to listen to *Edelweiss* or watch *The Poseidon Adventure* in triplicate. I wanted to see fields of fighting bulls, wave to goatherds with their lonely flocks, spy Moorish castles silhouetted against orange horizons… I didn't want transport; I wanted travel.

Fortunately, it will be many years before the cool, efficient modern Spain supplants the romantic, capricious Spain of tradition. But Spain is changing – and nowhere faster than in Andalusia. Under the aegis of Expo '92, the biggest construction site in Europe, the region is attempting to absorb in five years all the investment it would normally expect to receive in 30. Consequently our per-

ceptions of this over-sentimentalised part of Spain are changing too, with plenty of help from the men in marketing. While Andalusia will always be the birthplace of flamenco, the cradle of bullfighting, a playground for gypsy passion and the home of Spanish cliché, it is now to become the fashionable, hi-tech capital of southern Europe. Forget mantillas, matadors and donkey carts; think flamenco-rock, motorcycle Grand Prix and high-speed multi-screen trains.

Europe has already rediscovered Barcelona and Madrid; now we are being invited to savour another bold, confident Spanish city – Seville. Perhaps that's why you're heading there now, for Seville is indeed in a vibrant, fun-loving mood. During 1992 the city will be compulsive global viewing, host to the 20 million visitors expected at Expo '92. 'History is being made' the organisers claim. 'Money is being made' the cynics snipe. But the past augurs well for the present renaissance. Seville has already soared to one Golden Age, when the riches of the New World flowed through the city into Europe during the 16th century. Córdoba knew exceptional wealth and influence under the Moors when it became the exuberant, cosmopolitan capital of the Umayyad Caliphate in the 10th century. The Nasrid Kingdom of Granada attained majestic stature too, surviving in splendid isolation from the 13th to the 15th century.

Such flourishing times bequeathed to these three cities great monuments and cultural legacies that have long attracted travellers from afar. These are the principal subjects of this guide: the candle ends of history, the ruins of ancient empires, the relics of art for God's sake. They tell us many truths – that beauty is possible, that nothing lasts but plenty lingers. I hope this book helps you discover many more.

Nigel Tisdall

Itálica

Roman and Moorish Andalusia

The Río Guadalquivir is one of Spain's great rivers. Rising in the mountains of north-eastern Jaén, its waters wind west for some 375 miles (603.5km), carving an ever-widening valley that culminates in Las Marismas, the broad marshlands that stall its entry into the Atlantic beside the sherry town of Sanlúcar de Barrameda. Now bloated with silt, it is but a portly descendant of the fast-flowing, frequently-flooding Baetis (blessed) that the Romans knew. When their fleets arrived here in the 1st century BC they could sail upriver as far as Córdoba, a strategic point already colonised by Phoenician, Carthaginian and Iberian settlers.

The Romans laid the ground plan of southern Spain, building roads, bridges and aqueducts and establishing Córdoba, the home of Seneca and Lucan, as the capital of Hispania Ulterior. They redeveloped many of the prehistoric settlements bordering the Baetis, including Hispalis (now Seville), Carmona and Itálica. Rich archaeological finds have since been made in this vicinity, many of which now grace the museums and stately homes of Seville and Córdoba. Most famous of all is the Carambolo treasure in Seville's Museo Arqueológico, gold jewellery that testifies to the wealth of the kingdom of Tartessus that flourished here in the 8th and 9th centuries BC. Near Santiponce (now on the western outskirts of Seville) you can watch ballet performed amidst the crumbling ruins of Roman Itálica, birthplace of the emperors Trajan and Hadrian, while at Carmona a necropolis and amphitheatre survive.

With the fall of the Roman Empire, Spain came under the influence of the Visigoths who set up their capital in Toledo – some of their fountains, arches and columns can still be seen lurking in-

Culture

side Andalusian monuments constructed many centuries later. In AD 711 the Moors – principally Arabs and North African Berbers – landed at Tarifa. Their advance was phenomenal: within seven years they had conquered virtually all of the peninsula. What had begun as a daring foray was to result in eight centuries of Moorish rule and the flowering of one of Europe's greatest civilisations.

The Moors called their new land 'al-Andalus', and the river that fed it 'Guad-al-Quivir', the Great River. Córdoba was its capital – by the 10th century it had become the most important city in Europe, four times its present size, with a university, libraries, public baths, workshops, street-lighting and over a thousand mosques. The greatest of these, La Mezquita, still stands as a testimony to this golden age which reached its apogee with the construction of the palaces at Medinat al-Zahra (now Medina Azahara on the outskirts of Córdoba). Today their partly restored ruins barely hint at the opulence of this royal pleasure park which had its own zoo, mint, fabric factory and arsenal. At its centre stood a pool filled with mercury that when stirred sent the sunlight flashing round the surrounding marble patios, roofed with gold and silver tiles.

Fabulous wealth grew from the Moors' talent for irrigation in the rich lands of the Guadalquivir valley. The Greeks had introduced the vine and the olive – both cultivated intensively by the Romans – but it was the Arabs who added the orange and the almond tree, along with rice, aubergines, saffron, cotton, silk-farming, Moreno sheep and herbs, spices and fruits. They also, like the Phoenicians before them and the British long after, exploited the mineral resources of the surrounding sierras.

Medina Azahara

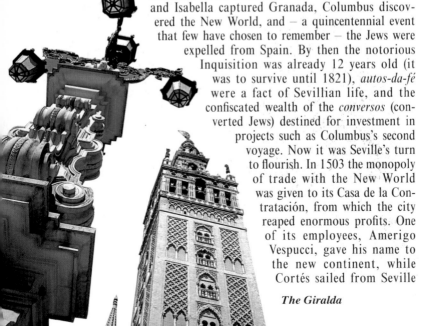

Moorish splendour

The Reconquest

Inevitably, it did not last. By the 11th century the refined glory of the Umayyad Caliphate had disintegrated into feuding *taifas* (factional kingdoms), easily overrun by the puritanical Almoravids whose Berber armies were summoned to prevent a Christian reconquest. They were in turn succeeded by the broader-minded Almohads who established their capital in Seville – the greatest of the *taifas* – and bequeathed us the Giralda and Torre del Oro as souvenirs of their reign.

In 1212 the Christians defeated the Almohads at Las Navas de Tolosa in the Sierra Morena, a turning point in the 700-year *Reconquista*. By 1236 Ferdinand III had captured Córdoba and 12 years later Seville fell. His success was aided by the complicity of the first Nasrid king, Ibn-al-Ahmar, who had retreated from Jaén to establish a power base in the mountains of the Sierra Nevada by taking over the former Almoravid capital of Granada.

By signing a peace treaty with the Christians, the kingdom of Granada – which roughly covered the modern provinces of Málaga, Granada and Almería – survived as a vassal state for the next 250 years. The city flourished as refugees and artisans from other captured cities arrived, enabling the introvert Nasrid kings to build what has become a poignant memorial to the swan-song days of al-Andalus, the Alhambra. At the same time a Christian king, Pedro the Cruel, was also employing Moorish craftsmen to build another tribute to this fading world – the Alcázar in Seville.

In 1492, one of those rare, watershed years when the whole world seems to shift on its axis, Ferdinand and Isabella captured Granada, Columbus discovered the New World, and – a quincentennial event that few have chosen to remember – the Jews were expelled from Spain. By then the notorious Inquisition was already 12 years old (it was to survive until 1821), *autos-da-fé* were a fact of Sevillian life, and the confiscated wealth of the *conversos* (converted Jews) destined for investment in projects such as Columbus's second voyage. Now it was Seville's turn to flourish. In 1503 the monopoly of trade with the New World was given to its Casa de la Contratación, from which the city reaped enormous profits. One of its employees, Amerigo Vespucci, gave his name to the new continent, while Cortés sailed from Seville

The Giralda

to ravage Mexico and Magellan to circumnavigate the globe. *Conquistadores* returned laden with gold and new found curiosities such as peppers, tomatoes, quinine and tobacco.

By 1588 Seville had a population of at least 80,000 and a stature equal to that of Venice. From here it embarked on a slow, glorious descent into decadence, a decline exacerbated by the expulsion of the *moriscos* (converted Moors) in 1610 and a great plague in 1649. During the 16th and 17th centuries Seville acted as a cosmopolitan transit point for trade, administration and emigration – its Lonja (Exchange), paid for by a quarter per cent tax on the import of silver, is now the Archive of the Indies where the signatures of these early colonisers are recorded.

These were heady, gold rush days of wealth and decay. Cervantes (1547–1616), who served time in Seville's prison, recorded its roguish underworld in his novels, while Murillo (1617–82) painted the beggared characters of its crowded streets. The Church, its coffers filled by the activities of the Inquisition, acquired a wealth that enabled it to build itself luxury city-centre sanctuaries that still force pedestrians to make boring circumnavigatory detours. At one point the city had over 70 convents, a glut only excused by the fact that they were often decorated by paintings and sculpture executed by artists such as Velázquez, Cano, Zurbarán, Murillo and Leal – all members of what is referred to now as the Seville School.

Bust of Cano, one of the Seville School of artists

In 1717 Seville received official recognition of its decline when the silting of the Guadalquivir forced the Casa de la Contratación to be moved south to Cádiz. Córdoba and Granada were now provincial backwaters in a demoralised Spain whose empire had been shrivelled by the War of the Spanish Succession (1701–14). In the course of the 18th and 19th centuries Andalusia became a romantic fiction to enchant Northern European audiences – the home

13

of gypsies, brigands, *majos* (dandies) and matadors. Seville was a city of aristocratic seducers called Don Juan and street-wise barbers called Figaro, while a gypsy girl by the name of Carmen worked in the sultry heat of its famous Tobacco Factory. In reality, Andalusia was a place of political chaos and poverty; by the start of the 19th century 72 per cent of the farming land in Seville was owned by an elite and invariably absentee landlord class that comprised barely five per cent of its population.

Travellers and Romantics

Poverty contributed to the appeal of southern Spain for the many aristocratic travellers who hired mules, boats and carriages to tour its provinces. They enjoyed its dilapidated state, exotic landscape and Moorish-Oriental heritage. The Alhambra – now a picturesque ruin where picaresque residents caught swallows with fishing rods – inspired much of this Romantic bliss. Washington Irving swam in its ancient pools, Théophile Gautier cooled sherry in its fountains and hotels appeared on the hill beside.

However, it was the comparatively passionate and openly sensual lifestyles of the Andalusians that really set northern hearts pumping. Hans Christian Andersen, visiting Andalusia in the 1860s, openly admitted his disappointment that he had not had 'just a little encounter with bandits'. One intrepid lady traveller, journeying to the Sahara at a similar time, confessed that after hearing a guitarist play in Granada 'you are ready to make love and war'.

Spain – which principally meant Andalusia – was in, a fashion encouraged by the victories of the Peninsular War (1809–14), its cheapness and the growth of trade interests such as sherry and mining. Granada and Seville topped the bill: 'Seville, the marvel of Andalusia, can be seen in a week' declared Richard Ford in his 1845 *Handbook for Spain*, a masterly work that did much to put Spain on the tourist map. Córdoba tended to receive, as it does now, a more perfunctory inspection.

By the end of the 19th century, Spain had lost virtually all of its remaining colonies and still lacked political stability. The nation remained neutral during World War I but in the 1920s became embroiled in a war of independence with its one-time masters, the Berber tribes of Morocco. In an attempt to create a lasting order out of chaos, General Miguel Primo de Rivera assumed power in a semi-dictatorship which had the concurrence of King Alfonso XIII: the pastiche pavilions built for the 1929 Ibero-American Exposition in Seville are a legacy of his period of power.

Carmen in stone

Columbus Was Everywhere

In 1485 Christopher Columbus (1451–1506) arrived in Spain to seek support for his 'Enterprise of the Indies' – a voyage that would try to reach the fabled shores of the East by sailing west across the Atlantic. Then aged 34, this Genoa-born mariner (who may have been of Spanish-Jewish descent) had prematurely white hair, was a widower with a five-year-old son, and had already sailed as far as Madeira, Iceland and the Gold Coast.

Columbus had just had his project turned down by the Portuguese court. He travelled to Córdoba in the spring of 1486 for an audience with Ferdinand and Isabella. The monarchs ordered a commission to assess his proposals which took four years to reach its damning verdict: 'vain and worthy of all rejection'. Columbus retreated to the monastery of La Rábida, near Huelva, but its prior, who had once been Isabella's confessor, succeeded in getting him recalled to the court.

His demands met, Columbus sailed on 3 August from Palos de la Frontera (near Huelva) with three caravels, *Nina*, *Pinta* and *Santa María*. On 12 October 1492 they sighted land – one of the Bahama Islands – and a few hours later the Spanish flag was planted in the New World.

Columbus made three more voyages. In 1493 he sailed from Cádiz and discovered Puerto Rico and Jamaica; in 1498 he sailed from Sanlúcar de Barrameda and reached the mouth of the Orinoco; finally in 1502 he sailed from Seville and discovered Panama.

In the last decade of his life he made frequent use of a Carthusian monastery to the west of Seville, Santa María de las Cuevas (La Cartuja, now the centrepoint of Expo '92). Here he wrote four autobiographical books, mourned the loss of his governorship over the lands he discovered, and hatched new plans – such as the liberation of Jerusalem.

Columbus died in Valladolid in 1506, after which the great discoverer's remains went on a mysterious voyage of their own. In 1509 they were brought back to La Cartuja, but were exhumed again in 1536 – perhaps being transferred to Seville's cathedral. Around 1544 they were shipped to the Caribbean island of Santo Domingo (now the Dominican Republic), but were later moved to Havana cathedral; then, in 1899, they were returned to Seville cathedral. What ended up where is anybody's guess, but one thing is certain: as the world goes quincentenary-mad an awful lot of places can stand up and say with all honesty 'Columbus was here'.

In the 1930s Ernest Hemingway wrote his paean to the noble art of bullfighting, *Death in the Afternoon*, and many artists and intellectuals volunteered their support for the Republican cause during the Spanish Civil War (1936–9). Seville, Córdoba and Granada were among the first cities to be taken by Franco's Nationalist forces at the start of this war. Up to a million people died, including many executed in these cities in the first days. One of them was the Granada-born poet and dramatist, Federico García Lorca.

In the aftermath of World War II, during which Spain remained neutral, the country was left isolated and impoverished. Franco's dictatorship lasted until his death in 1975, a period of steady economic advance scarred by political and cultural repression. Many Andalusians migrated to the northern industrial cities or abroad, leaving the countryside deserted. Franco's acceptance in 1953 of American military bases in exchange for loans, along with Spain's subsequent admission to the UN, accelerated its economic recovery and led to the development of mass tourism on its Mediterranean coast during the 1960s.

In 1975, monarchy returned in the shape of King Juan Carlos, soon to be followed by democratic elections. In 1982 the Socialist PSOE party, led by charismatic Sevillian lawyer Felipe González, won a sweeping victory. Critics say that the country has since been hijacked by a *sevillano* mafia; others protest that the current investment in the region is long overdue. What's clear is that Andalusia is already playing a major role in Spain's rapid regeneration, with Seville staging the Universal Exposition in 1992 and Granada hosting the World Alpine Ski Championships in 1995.

And yet, for all the multi-million-peseta *proyectos* and hi-tech facelifts scribbled on the countryside in the name of Expo, the romantic, rose-in-the-teeth view of Andalusia persists. Not just in the tourist brochures and souvenir stalls but casually fostered by the Andalusians themselves in their patios, bars, *peñas* (clubs) and *ferias* (fairs). In the countryside, donkeys still plough the fields. Andalusia will always be Spain spiced with the exotic tang of North Africa, a mountain-locked land racked by relentless summer heat and fed by the lazy waters of the Guadalquivir.

Artesanado ceiling work

Historical Outline

BC

c.10,000 Cave paintings at La Pileta (near Ronda) show there were prehistoric settlers in Andalusia during Palaeolithic times.

2,000–500 The kingdom of Tartessus flourishes in the area around Seville; trading links with the Greeks are established.

1100 The Phoenicians found Gadir (Cádiz).

3rd century Carthaginian forces conquer Andalusia.

218 Roman colonisation of Spain begins with the Second Punic War.

1st century BC–3rd century AD The Romans transform Andalusia, developing its agriculture and constructing roads and aqueducts. Itálica, Carmona and Seville are founded; Córdoba becomes the capital of Hispania Ulterior.

AD

400–500 Spain is dominated by the Visigoths.

711 Moorish armies cross the Straits of Gibraltar, conquering the peninsula within seven years.

756–1031 Umayyad dynasty rules over al-Andalus. Córdoba emerges as the capital of Muslim Spain; work starts on La Mezquita. In 929, Abd ar-Rahman III proclaims caliphate of Córdoba.

1086 The Almoravids, fundamentalist Muslim Berbers, invade Spain. They are expelled in 1147 by the Almohads who build the Great Mosque of Seville, crowned by a minaret, La Giralda.

1212 The Almohads are defeated at the Battle of Las Navas de Tolosa. By 1248, Ferdinand III has taken both Córdoba and Seville.

1237–1492 Nasrid dynasty rules the Kingdom of Granada. Construction of the Alhambra. In the 1360s Pedro the Cruel builds Seville's Alcázar; work starts on the cathedral in 1401.

1469 Marriage of Ferdinand V to Isabella I unites the kingdoms of Aragón and Castile.

1492 Fall of Granada; Columbus discovers America.

1500s Seville is granted a trade monopoly with the New World. In 1520s work begins on the cathedral in Córdoba's Mezquita, on Granada cathedral, and Charles V's palace in the Alhambra.

1600s Prosperity turns to decadence. Seville declines as the Guadalquivir silts up and trade moves to Cádiz. The city produces some of Spain's greatest artists.

1759–88 Charles III introduces enlightened reforms; Seville's Tobacco Factory is completed.

1809–14 Seville, Córdoba and Granada occupied by the French during the Peninsular War.

1800s Spain struggles for political stability and loses its colonies. Romantic travellers discover the region.

1929 Ibero-American Exposition held in Seville.

1936–9 Spanish Civil War: Seville, Córdoba and Granada occupied by Nationalists, parts of eastern Andalusia held by Republicans.

1975 Franco dies; Juan Carlos I becomes king.

1982 Spain elects a socialist government led by Sevillian Felipe González. Andalusia is granted new autonomous powers.

1986 Spain joins the European Community (EC).

1992 Seville stages Expo '92; Barcelona hosts Summer Olympics; Madrid is Cultural Capital of Europe. Quincentenary of Columbus's discovery of America.

Seville

400 m / 0.25 miles

1 Cathedral
2 Reales Alcázares and Gardens
3 Archivo General de Indias
4 Torre del Oro
5 Maestranza bullring
6 Hospital de la Caridad
7 Casa de Pilatos
8 Convento San Leandro
9 Plaza Alfalfa
10 Plaza del Salvador

- ● - ● = Itinerary 1
- ● - ● = Itinerary 2
- ● - ● = Itinerary 3

Río Guadalquivir

Puente de la Barqueta
Resolana
Becquer
Calatrava
Peral
Feria
Relator
Macasta
Castellar

Pasarela de la Cartuja

Torneo
San Vicente
Sta. Ana
Gran Poder
Jesús
Amor de Dios

Pascual de Gayangos
Banos
Gíoles
Torneo

Alfonso XII Campana
Museo de Bellas Artes

Marqués de Paradas
Canalejas
M. Núñez
Velázquez Tetuán
Sierpes
A. Quintero

Almansa
Zaragoza

Av. Cristo de la Expiración
JARDINES DE CHAPINA

Castilla
Puente de Isabel II
Betis
Paseo de Cristóbal Colón

Pages del Corro
San Jacinto

Triana

Evangelista
Leiria
Pages del Corro
Troya
Febo
Arolla

Trabajo
V. de Fátima

República Argentina
Asunción
Virgen
Turia
del Valle

V. de Aguas Santas

Turia
Virgen de Luján

PARQUE DE LOS PRINCIPES

Virgen del Aguila
Fernando IV
Asunción

Av. Ramón de Carranza
Joselito El Gallo
Pascual Márquez

Don Fadrique
Macarena
San Juan de Ribera
Fray Isidoro de Sevilla
León XIII
M. Villalobos
Dr. J. Díaz
Ronda de Pío XIII
Alhelí

Basílica Macarena

Feria
Parras
San Luis

Pl. del Cronista

Alda. de la Cruz Roja
Avenida de Miraflores
Carr. de Carmona

Ronda de Capuchinos

Pl. del Pelicano
Sol

Arroyo
Carr. de S.J. Bosco

Alameda de Hércules

S. Lorenzo y Jesús del Gran Poder

JARDINES DEL VALLE

Bustos Tavera
Sol

M. Auñilladora
Arroyo

José Laguillo

Sta. Catalina

Imagen
Azafrán
Santiago
Navarros

Amador de los Ríos
Campo de los Mártires

Palacio Lebrija

Estrella
Aldoliga

⑨

⑩

Plaza Nueva

G. el Bueno

C. Ibarra

Pl. de las Mercedarias

⑧

⑦

Juan A. Cavestany

Luis Montoto

Pirineos

Pl. Triunfo
① ③

Pl. D. Elvira

②

Pl. Sta. Cruz

y Pelayo

Demetrio de los R.

Puente de S. Bernardo

Avenida de E. Dato

Jiménez Aranda

San Bernardo

Teatro de la Maestranza

⑤

Valflora

⑥
④

Alm. Lobo

Puerta de Jerez

Av. G. Sanjurjo
Av. de Roma

Pl. de la Contratación

San Fernando

Avenida Menéndez y Pelayo

Av. de Cádiz
Av. de Málaga

Campamento

Puente San Telmo
Pl. Cuba

Juan Sebastián Elcano
Avenida de las Delicias
Alfonso XIII

Universidad

Pl. de D. Juan de Austria

Av. de Carlos V

Cruz Conde

Av. de Portugal

JARDINES DE S. TELMO

Av. de María Luisa

Av. Rodríguez de Caso

Av. de la Borbolla

Dr. Pedro de Castro

Arcos

Puente del Generalísimo

Plaza de España

San Salvador

Parque de

María Luisa

Porvenir

Almirante Topete

Av. de Carreo Blanco

Museo de Artes y Costumbre Populares

Avenida Felipe II

Museo Arqueológico

Colombia

Bogota

Puente de Alfonso XIII

Av. Eritana

Costillares

Seville

'Let us build a church,' mused the architects of Seville cathedral, 'so big that we shall be held to be insane.' And they did – a vainglorious feat that now squats in the city centre like an obstinate bag-lady. The cathedral, and particularly its great Moorish tower, La Giralda, is Seville's best known landmark, and worth the climb if only to help orientate yourself in what at first seems a hopeless jumble of narrow streets.

Seville has been conducting a long-standing love affair with the grandiose. Next-door to the cathedral you will find Pedro the Cruel's splendid Alcázar, inspired by the Alhambra and later enlarged by Charles V. South of this stands the immense Tobacco Factory, second only to the Escorial in size. Beyond are the expansive remains of the great pavilions, plazas and parks built for the Ibero-American Exposition that almost bankrupted the city in 1929.

You may well judge Seville to be insane (the traffic certainly is) but it has an endearing panache too – most obvious in the city's intense celebration of Semana Santa (Holy Week) and the exuberant Feria (April Fair) that follows it. Such style and energy will be in evidence when Seville leads the 1992 quincentennial celebrations of the Discovery of America, in Expo '92. Preparations for this massive exhibition have already transformed the city: six new bridges, a spanking new railway station, an expanded airport, new ring-roads, a new theatre, whole *barrios* restored. *Mira al futuro* the billboards coo, and indeed the future does look good.

And yet Seville somehow remains a quiet and intimate city at heart, sensual and faintly decadent, where people live well: sipping their *fino*, washing their *patio* floors, *paseo*-ing four-abreast with triple-decker ice creams. It's such qualities that will make you come back here long after the builders' dust has been swept away.

Seville: the cathedral and Giralda

1. Cathedral and Parque de María Luisa

Around the immense cathedral and up the Giralda, its Moorish minaret, for a view of the city. Lunch, and then on foot past where Carmen worked to the venue for Seville's 1929 exhibition, the Parque de María Luisa.

Breakfast in Seville is a brisk, private affair – perhaps a *café con leche* and some *tostada* smeared with olive oil or fish paste, taken standing at the bar in a mood of pensive solemnity. **Bar Los Principes** (Calle Arfe 7) evokes this big city mood admirably, while **Bar**

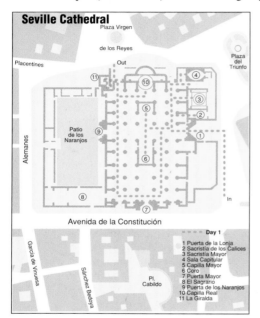

Seville Cathedral

Plaza Virgen de los Reyes

Plaza del Triunfo

Placentines

Out

Alemanes

Patio de los Naranjos

García de Viñuesa

Sánchez Bedoya

Pl. Cabildo

Avenida de la Constitución

In

- - - - **Day 1**
1 Puerta de la Lonja
2 Sacristía de los Cálices
3 Sacristía Mayor
4 Sala Capitular
5 Capilla Mayor
6 Coro
7 Puerta Mayor
8 El Sagrario
9 Puerta de los Naranjos
10 Capilla Real
11 La Giralda

Ibense, on the junction of Avenida de la Constitución and Calle Almirantazgo, is the ideal place for a quick *café* before you tackle Seville's monster cathedral (open Monday–Friday 11am –5pm, Saturday 11am–4pm, Sunday 2–4pm).

The **Cathedral Santa María de la Sede** began life in 1401 and occupies the former site of a great mosque built by the Almohads in 1172 – its immense size clearly results from the Christian architects' desire to trump the grandeur of their 'heathen' predecessors. A century later it had grown to become the biggest Gothic cathedral in the world – only St Paul's in London and St Peter's in Rome are larger. Inevitably, on first arriving in Seville, you will have passed its rambling exterior, surrounded by enchained Roman pillars taken from Itálica. The adjoining steps, **Las Gradas,** were for many centuries Seville's main meeting-place.

If you're crossing from the Bar Ibense be sure to look up as you wait (and wait) for the lights to change – above the cathedral you will have a clear view of **La Giralda** and the silhouette of its crowning weather-vane (*giraldillo*), a revolving bronze statue of Faith which was added in the 16th century. The main *entrada* is ahead on the cathedral's southern façade (before 11am and at weekends various other doors are opened; this itinerary follows the weekday one-way system). Don't be dismayed by the tourist queues, because the more people that enter this leviathan, the better. Passing through the Puerta de la Lonja, only completed at the start of this century, you are immediately confronted by the oversized tomb of Christopher Columbus, supported by four pallbearers represent-

Detail from the cathedral door

ing the kingdoms of Castile, León, Aragón and Navarre (see 'Columbus Was Everywhere' in the *History and Culture* section).

Ahead you can't fail to see the *coro* (choir) and Capilla Mayor (main chapel), while the shadowy depths of the cathedral's cavernous interior stretch to the left. Before braving the gloom turn right to inspect a series of side rooms housing religious treasures.

Beyond the chapel of Los Dolores is the Sacristía de los Calices: amongst its disgracefully-lit works of art you'll encounter a common anachronistic depiction – this one by Goya – of the Giralda and two 3rd-century Sevillian martyrs, Santa Justa and Santa Rufina, who escaped death in the lions' den. Next door is the Sacristía Mayor with more sacrilegiously-displayed works by Zurbarán, Murillo and van Dyck, along with some of the venerated relics that are paraded through the streets during Semana Santa. Right in the far corner of the cathedral, next to rooms exhibiting clerical vestments and illuminated manuscripts, a curved passage leads to the Sala Capitular, an elliptical room with an *Immaculate Conception* by Murillo.

Returning to the centre of the cathedral, take a pew to study the **Capilla Mayor**'s huge **retablo**, a deluge of gold that was begun in 1482 by the Flemish sculptor Pieter Dancart – and completed 82 years later. From here you can stumble around the vast interior (clockwise). At the far end is the huge, rarely-opened Puerta Mayor and in the next corner the original statue of Faith that capped La Giralda until it was replaced by a copy. Behind this is El Sagrario, the Tabernacle Chapel – in effect a church within a church where many Sevillians prefer to attend mass (access from the Avenida de la Constitución). Wandering on, you will realise that the cathedral is virtually a city within a city, terraced with side chapels, adorned with statues and tombs, full of dusty cor-

The Giralda

Ceramic from the city of oranges

ners housing long-forgotten memorials.

When you've had enough gloom turn left through the Puerta de los Naranjos into a large *patio* lined with orange trees. A legacy of the original mosque, it seems inconceivable that this peaceful courtyard, which has a Visigothic fountain at its centre, became a notorious sanctuary for criminals in the 16th century. Returning indoors you will find that the exit for climbing La Giralda lies ahead. Before you leave continue round to view the Capilla Real, dedicated to the Virgen de los Reyes, where a silver urn contains the relics of Ferdinand III (who expelled the Moors from Seville and Córdoba); nearby are the tombs of his wife Beatrice and son Alfonso X (The Wise).

La Giralda is a Moorish minaret capped with a Christian belfry – the ultimate *Reconquista* symbol. Climbing it is like watching a slide show of the city – 34 ramps and a flight of steps later you emerge beneath its awesome bells for a glorious view over Seville. Here you'll find not only a classic Andalusian skyline of whitewashed houses and terracotta-tiled roofs, for centuries pierced only by the domes and bell-towers of the city's multitude of churches and convents, but also the new-money monuments that have recently transformed the city. To the west, beyond the bullring, are the new bridges to Expo '92 (including the brilliant wishbone arch of La Puente de la Barqueta) and the Banesto Tower; to the east is the futuristic new railway station, Santa Justa.

Bells in the Giralda

After all that death and work you'll be ready for life and lunch – head straight for the **Cervecería Giralda** (Calle Mateos Gago 1) which has plenty of both. This lies straight ahead from the Cathedral exit, across the **Plaza Virgen de los Reyes**. If you arrive before 1.30pm you should be able to get a table in this busy *tapas* bar – look on the blackboard for the *raciones* on offer that day, which normally include typical Sevillian dishes like *huevos a la flamenca* (eggs with ham and vegetables) and *cazuela Tio Pepe* (casserole with sherry). For a more upstage meal consider the **El Giraldillo** restaurant – it is touristy and expensive but then the view from its tables is priceless. Whatever you choose, do linger a moment in the Plaza de los Virgen Reyes – even more romantic at night when its monumental lamp-post is lit.

In the afternoon your itinerary leads idly towards the shady bliss of the Parque de María Luisa. If you prefer, you can ride there in style by horse and carriage – there are several *coches de caballos* ranks around the cathedral. Negotiate a price first – if you want to know the going rate ask in the Tourist Office (just round the corner at

Tourist transport to the park

Avenida de la Constitución 21: roughly 2,500 pesetas per hour at the time of writing). Otherwise continue back towards the cathedral entrance, turning left into the Plaza del Triunfo where a column celebrates Seville's survival of the 1755 earthquake that devastated Lisbon. Continue back to Avenida del Constitución and turn left – en route you will pass the back of the Lonja and the entrance to the Reales Alcázares (see Itinerary 2).

Avenida de la Constitución culminates in the Puerta de Jerez and a Grand Prix of traffic. Bear left around this roundabout to reach a luxury oasis, the **Hotel Alfonso XIII.** Opened in 1928, the hotel formed part of an audacious ensemble of neo-Moorish, pro-Andalusian, *azulejo*-covered buildings constructed for the 1929 Ibero-American Exposition. A celebration of all things Spanish and Spanish-American, Expo '29 took some 15 years to build but ended in

Whispering statues in the Parque de María Luisa

anti-climax: Seville was left with enormous debts. None of this seems to worry the hotel's wealthy clientele, however; pop in for a drink in the bar (12am–1am), or for a look at its grand patio.

Continue along Calle San Fernando to the great hulk of the **Real Fábrica de Tabacos**, completed in 1757, which is now part of Seville's University. It is possible to take a short-cut through the building (straight through the centre), which still bears a few signs and name-plates left from the days when it employed thousands of young *cigarerras* to roll cigars. Some accounts suggest that 12,000 young girls worked here – the prospect clearly intoxicated the minds of many Romantic male travellers who came to Seville. Amongst these was Prosper Mérimée, a French writer whose story about one of the workforce, *Carmen*, inspired Bizet's famous opera.

If you walk through or round the building you'll arrive at a junction where a statue of the *Reconquista* hero El Cid attempts to control the traffic. Skirt round it, past the Teatro Lope de Vega and into the Avenida Isabel la Católica. The towers of the **Plaza de España**, inspired by Santiago de Compostela, will guide you.

The Plaza, in keeping with Seville's desire to build every monument bigger than the last, is enormous. It once housed the Spanish Pavilion but is now an obsolete, *azulejo*-crazed playground. Enjoy it, and the rest of the adjacent **Parque de María Luisa**. Its rambling and mature gardens were once part of the grounds adjoining the baroque San Telmo Palace. Assorted Romantic statuary inhabits the undergrowth while further south you'll find two more pavilions in the Plaza de América (see 'Museums' itinerary).

Plaza de España

When you've had enough cut through to the riverside Avenida de las Delicias. 'How pleasant to stroll along the shore of the Guadalquivir in a grove called Las Delicias', wrote George Borrow in 1842. It's a highway now, but at least that means you can hail a taxi back.

24

2. La Maestranza and Reales Alcázares

To the bullring via the Archivo General de Indias. Inspect the paintings in the Hospital built by the original Don Juan. After a liquid lunch, lose yourself in the magnificent Reales Alcázares and gardens.

The centre of Seville is neatly split in two by the Avenida de la Constitución. To the east is the Cathedral and the Barrio Santa Cruz – the old Jewish quarter that was smartened up in the 1920s and has been metamorphosing into a picturesque tourist ghetto ever since. To the west lies El Arenal, a web of quiet, unpretentious streets centred on Seville's bullring, La Maestranza.

Before exploring this area, visit the **Archivo General de Indias** (open Monday–Saturday 10am–1pm), in the heavyweight Lonja next to the cathedral. Formerly the stock exchange, the Lonja was designed in 1584 by Juan de Herrera, architect of Madrid's massive El Escorial. Since the 1750s it has been a records office for all the documents relating to the discovery and colonisation of the New World. A few of the thousands of millions of papers stored here are always out on display in the exhibition rooms up the grand stairs – perhaps a street-plan of Buenos Aires in 1713, a sketch of Inca weapons or a watercolour map of a fort in Florida.

From the Lonja cross over Avenida de la Constitución and turn right then left into Calle Almirantazgo. Here an archway to the right of the Café Los Pinelos will take you into the little-visited **Plaza del Cabildo**, scene of a collectors' market on Sundays. Look for a small shop, El Torno, which sells delicious cakes and biscuits made by the various convents in and around Seville – a good chance to buy something to nibble when you visit the Royal Palaces this afternoon. From here you can take a passage past the

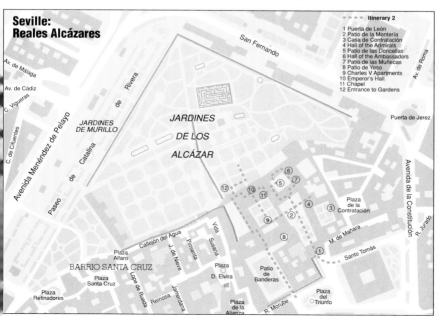

Seville: Reales Alcázares

Itinerary 2
1 Puerta de León
2 Patio de la Montería
3 Casa de Contratación
4 Hall of the Admirals
5 Patio de las Doncellas
6 Hall of the Ambassadors
7 Patio de las Muñecas
8 Patio de Yeso
9 Charles V Apartments
10 Emperor's Hall
11 Chapel
12 Entrance to Gardens

Figon del Cabildo restaurant into Calle Arfe. Immediately in front of you is El Postigo, a municipal arts and crafts market.

Turn right, continuing down Calle Arfe and left into Calle Antonio Díaz. The junction of streets here is a good point to return to in the evening if you're looking for an easy-going place for dinner. Straight ahead is the popular Mesón Sevilla Jabugo II and opposite a take-away *freiduría* (fried fish shop – only open evenings).

Round the corner El Buzo (open all night) and Bar Mesón Serranito both serve Sevillian dishes in a bull-fighter's ambience. Heading back to the cathedral, Bodegas Diaz Salazar in Calle García de Vinuesa is friendly and has a good pinball machine.

At the bottom of Calle Antonio Díaz is La Maestranza – even if bullfighting isn't your cup of blood you have to admit that Seville's **Plaza de Toros** is an impressive piece of architecture (Monday–Saturday 10am–1.30pm). Built in 1760, it is one of the oldest and most prestigious bullrings in Spain. It's well worth taking a guided tour (30 mins), which includes a visit to its museum, matadors'

Arches in the Reales Alcázares

chapel and stables. If you would like to attend a *corrida* then 'Bullfights' in the *Entertainment* section will tell you how.

From La Maestranza you can cross the road to the banks of the Río Guadalquivir – renamed the Canal de Alfonso XIII since 1948 when the river was diverted further west to prevent flooding. (The river will be re-opened for Expo '92, enabling visitors to cruise around the Isla de la Cartuja, the exhibition venue.) Across the river to the north you'll see an iron bridge (1852) crossing over to Triana, the traditional gypsy quarter of Seville. A blue-collar neighbourhood where most of Seville's dockers and watermen lived, Triana has a completely different atmosphere and is worth visiting to enjoy its shops and markets or its lively bars and nightlife.

Turn left to walk down the pleasant Paseo de Cristóbal Colón. Ahead you will see the 13th century **Torre del Oro**, built by the Al-

The Torre del Oro

mohads to anchor a great chain that stretched across the river to defend the city. Today it contains a museum of nautical curiosities (Tuesday–Friday 10am–2pm, Saturday and Sunday 10am–1pm, closed Monday). From here you can take sightseeing bus tours of the city and cruises down the Guadalquivir.

Before you reach the tower cross back over the road and walk past the gardens of the spanking new opera house, the Teatro de La Maestranza, opened in May 1991 (Calle Nuñez de Balboa). At the end you will find the **Hospital de la Caridad** (Monday–Saturday 10am–1pm and 3.30–6pm, Sunday 10.30am–12.30pm). Founded in 1674, the building is still used as a charity hospital but is also open to the public. Apart from its exquisite patio, the Hospital has a chapel (to the left) that exemplifies the great patronage of the arts pursued by such institutions during Seville's Golden Age. Here you will find two ghoulish works by Valdés Leal (above the door and opposite) and several paintings by Murillo. Four of the best were pillaged by Marshal Soult in 1810.

Leaving the Hospital you will see a statue of its founder **Don Miguel de Mañara**, considered by some to be the role model for Don Juan, the cynical lover who had 1,003 Spanish mistresses. Decide for yourself if this man looks like a reformed seducer or a repentant Don Giovanni. The Hospital became a point of call for Romantic visitors who believed Seville to be the hot-bed of the lascivious South. Byron explained why in his own *Don Juan*: 'What men call gallantry, and gods adultery, / Is much more common where the climate's sultry.' Such contentious matters are best discussed over a glass of *fino*, which can be found in the cavernous **Bodegón del Torre del Oro** round the corner (turn left into Calle Santander). If you like sherry this is a good place to try some *manzanilla* or the stronger *oloroso*. The Bodegón also serves typical *raciones* such as *espinacas de garbanzos* (spinach with chick-peas) and *cola de toro* (bull's tail).

Suitably fortified, you now take on the **Reales Alcázares** (Tuesday–Saturday 10.30am–5.30pm, Sunday 10am–1.30 pm, closed Monday). The entrance to these Royal Palaces is in the

Plaza del Triunfo to the east of the cathedral – straight up Calle Santander and Calle Santo Tomás. The Reales Alcázares are Pedro the Cruel's contribution to Seville's majestic monuments. For a Castilian king (1350–69) with a reputation for barbaric behaviour, it is surprising to find his palatial residences such a fulsome homage to the refined abstraction of Islam. Pedro, who adopted Arab dress and filled his court with Moorish entertainers, exemplifies how the Reconquest monarchs fell in love with what they had just destroyed. Ironically he had little time to enjoy his Alcázar – he was murdered three years after its completion.

You enter through the Puerta de León – close by are some castellated walls left over from the Almohad fortress that previously stood here. Inside you quickly discover that the Palaces have undergone considerable alteration since the 14th century. Passing through some small gardens you'll arrive in a large courtyard, the **Patio de la Montería**. Here you will find the work of Charles V, who added a whole set of **Royal Apartments** to the left. To the right is the **Casa de la Contratación**, the work of Ferdinand and Isabella, an establishment which had the monopoly on all trade with the New World for over a century. Inside you'll find the Hall

Pavilion in the Alcázar gardens

THE CATHEDRAL
OF SEVILLE

The tower of the old mosque (Aljama) was finished in 1198 and the belffry in 1568.

When coming down from the tower and entering the Cathedral again, where the walk has no architectural barriers, you will have a general view of the gothic building, made up of five naves of nine sections each, a line of chapels on each side, and another one at the head near you.

In the central nave, there are two "Buildings": The Choir (you cannot see it from here) and the Main Chapel, placed just in front of you. These additions open three "transversal areas": "The nave of the main chapel", "The transept" (placed at the entrance where the vaults are the highest in the whole Cathedral) and finally the "Choir". Each one belonged to one three hierarchic soad classes during the Sevillian Mediaeval age: The Royal, Ecclesiastical and popular.

This Gothic Cathedral was begun in 1401, perhaps at the beginning of summer, and was finished in 1519.

You have already notice the Cathedral is made of stone meanwhile the mosque was made of brick.

The graded vaults whose height from the central span of the transept (Choir area, is 37 m from the ground to the keystone and unique with decorated

vaults) and the four "minors" naves and the Main Chapel (24,50 m) to the periphery of the chapels on the sides.

From here, you can do the rest of the visit as you wish, but if you don't want to miss any space or any of the pieces of art, we suggest you follow the itinerary appears on the plan marked by arrows.

In general, the access to the chapels, choir and dependances is forbbiden, except toilets which are perfectly indicated and the area that surrounds the two sacristies and the Chapter where you find yourself near the end of your visit.

The construction of the final area you see is the most modern part, started in 1509 (Sacristía de los Cálices), continuing with the Major Sacristy and the Court of "Oleos" (1529-1543) and completed when the chapter room was decorated, the last of the important pieces you will visit before going out through the door of "De la Campanilla".

At the moment this free guide is being prepared, the complet itinerary is at your disposal, but it might be that you find some restricted areas, due to some ceremonies, masses, restorations work, and so on.

We ask for your pardon, and are grateful for your colaboration and understanding.

Azulejo from the Emperor's Hall

of the Admirals – used for planning naval expeditions – and beyond it a chapel with a starlit *artesanado* ceiling.

Ahead rises the exterior façade of Pedro's pleasure-dome. Inside (bear left) you pass through a vestibule to suddenly enter its opulent centre, the **Patio de las Doncellas** (Maids). Much of the Alcázar's decoration was probably executed by the craftsmen who worked on Granada's Alhambra; Seville's Christian rulers allowed them to incorporate Koranic inscriptions into the intricate tiles and stucco but had their own mottos and coats-of-arms added. The upper storey is a 16th century addition but the courtyard is still impressive – inevitably the *azulejos* steal the show.

Continuing straight ahead you enter the **Salón de Carlos V** with its fine coffered ceiling, followed by (turn right) three rooms that once belonged to Pedro the Cruel's mistress, María de Padilla. Turning the corner brings you into the **Salón de los Embajadores** (Ambassadors). The cedar cupola was added in 1427 and restored and embellished in subsequent centuries, but the room, with its triple arcade of horseshoe arches, is resoundingly Moorish. Parallel to this room is Philip II's dining room and ahead his bedroom – perhaps the sober wooden ceiling, such a contrast to the fireworks and starbursts elsewhere, was installed to help him get to sleep.

Next you enter the small **Patio de las Muñecas** (Dolls) – named after a pair of doll's heads somewhere in the decoration... The upper floor is a mid-19th century 'enhancement'. To the left is Isabella the Catholic's bedroom, and ahead that of her only son, Don Juan. To the right is the **Salón de los Reyes Moros** (Moorish Kings).

Back in the Patio de la Montería turn right into an arcade; to the left, beyond an iron grille, lies the oldest part of the Alcázar, including the Patio de Yeso that has survived from the 12th century Almohad palace (unfortunately closed). Continue through the gardens to the **Charles V Apartments** – first comes a room of Flemish tapestries depicting Charles's campaigns in Tunisia, followed by the Emperor's Hall and Chapel. Here the bright yellow *azulejos*, bursting with avaricious birds, snake-entwined cherubs and general Renaissance japery, make a refreshing change to the meditative geometrics of Islamic interior design. Their comic relief is an ideal introduction to the Alcázar's gardens that follow – a rambling paradise of box hedges and citrus groves mined with pools, pavilions and fountains, just the place to get lost in.

3. City Walk via Casa de Pilatos

This afternoon walk rambles through the some of the prettiest back streets of Seville, calling in at the very desirable Casa de Pilatos, an early 16th century palace that achieves a remarkable synthesis of Moorish and Renaissance spirits. It ends in Calle Sierpes, the city's principal shopping street. If you start at about 4pm on a weekday you should arrive in Sierpes when the 'paseo' is in full swing and its shops and cafés bubbling with life.

The walk starts in the **Patio de las Banderas** (Flags) – where you exit from the Reales Alcázares. An archway in the far corner will take you into the narrow streets of the Barrio Santa Cruz. After the covered alley bear left into Calle Vida. Leave via the long Callejón del Aqua which ends in the Plaza de Alfaro: steps to the right lead down to the **Murillo Gardens**. Continue ahead (bear left) into the Plaza de Santa Cruz, framed by Sevillian mansions with a 17th century iron cross in the centre. Further on, Calle Mezquita takes you to the Plaza del Refinadores (Polishers), overseen by a haughty statue of Don Juan.

Look for a small alley (by Calle Mariscon 9) that will take you up to the Plaza de Cruces (Crosses), and another continuing straight on. At the top turn right into Calle Ximénez de Enciso, and when it ends go left towards the Hotel Fernando III for Calle Cespedes. This winds through (bear left) to the cobbled Plaza de las Mercederías, fronted by a huge red-brick convent. Take Calle Vidrio until it becomes pedestrianised, turning left (by No 25) into a tiny alley, the encouragingly-named Calle Cristo del Buen Viaje. This delivers you to the incongruously-named Bar Malawi – turn left (Calle San Esteban) towards the restful **Plaza de Pilatos** where a statue of Zurbarán will greet

From the Callejón del Agua

you. If you think the great painter looks a bit annoyed it's probably because someone has stolen his paintbrush.

The **Casa de Pilatos** (daily 9am–6pm) is said to have been modelled on Pontius Pilate's house in Jerusalem after its creator, the Marquis of Tarifa, had paid a visit to the Holy Land. Completed in 1540, it is decorated in Mudéjar style but has none of the intro-

The Plaza de Cruces

version and claustrophobia found in Pedro the Cruel's earlier Alcázar. Instead it is spacious and eclectic, a delightul combination of Italianate grace and Arab artistry. You enter first through a Roman-style triumphal arch, crossing the *apeadero* (carriage yard) to its central patio where arcades of Moorish arches are echoed by Gothic ones on the floor above.

This courtyard contains some of the finest *azulejos* you will ever see – dazzling, puzzle-book patterns in brilliant colours that include some extraordinary quasi-Impressionist designs. The Roman statuary was imported from Italy. If you walk to the right, through the Praetorian Chamber, you will discover a small garden. Continuing round the patio (anti-clockwise), you'll encounter the Chapel and Pilate's Study, which open onto enchanting gardens blessed with trickling fountains and cascading bougainvillea. A monumental staircase further round leads up to a late Mudéjar cupola (1537) that could have been inspired by a Ferrero Rocher chocolate. Here you can take a rather abrupt guided tour of the upstairs apartments, packed with art treasures acquired over the centuries by the palace's aristocratic owners (parts of the house are still used by the Medinaceli family).

When you leave, turn right to walk past the Hostal Atenas (Calle Caballerizas) to reach the ochre and amber façade of the Baroque Iglesia de San Ildefonso. Directly opposite is a brown metal door leading into the **Convento San Leandro**, a closed-order convent where you can buy – via a brass-studded revolving drum – its fa-

Inside the Casa de Pilatos

Church of El Salvador

mous *yemas* (see 'Heavenly Sweets' in *Eating Out*).

Leave the adjacent plaza by the far corner, where Calle Boteros winds through via Calle Odreros to the **Plaza Alfalfa**, scene of an easy-going pet market on Sunday mornings. If you're ready for a drink or a snack, the Horno San Buenaventura patisserie is a must for anyone who considers cake-choosing a serious art-form. From here you can take the narrow Calle Alcaicería de la Loza (by the Bar Ibense sign) into Seville's extensive pedestrian shopping area. First you will meet the Plaza de Jesús de la Passion – devoted almost entirely to shops selling wedding dresses – and then the popular **Plaza del Salvador**. Between the two sits the fat church of El Salvador, built mostly in the 17th century.

The Plaza del Salvador sits half-way up a ladder of shopping streets running north-south. These are best explored at whim, but a good circuit is up to the top of Calle Cuna, left and then back down Seville's main strolling and spending artery, Calle Sierpes. While passing along Calle Cuna look out for the Casa de la Condesa de Lebrija (at No 8), another Sevillian stately home with a grand patio and stunning mosaics filched from Itálica (Monday and Friday only, 5–7pm; closed August). At the top of Calle Sierpes La Campana (No 1) is one of the best cake shops in Seville if not Spain. At the southern end of this serpentine street you'll find the **Plaza Nueva** and the wonderful Plateresque façade of Seville's old Ayuntiamento (1564) – beyond this is the Avenida de la Constitución and the cathedral.

For dining consider the restaurants around the north of Calle Sierpes such as **El Bacalao** (Plaza Ponce de León 15, Tel: 421 66 70) which specialises in codfish, or its expensive new cousin **Las Columnas de Baco** (Calle Santa María de Gracía 2, Tel: 421 51 51), useful if you want to escape the grime of the streets; if you eat at the bar it's a lot cheaper. For a trendy example of the New Seville it's worth seeking out **Restaurante Parabere** (Narciso Campillo 4, Tel: 456 09 03; closed Sunday), in a side-street off Calle Santas Patrona. The **Bar Alfonso Rey de Los Caracoles** nearby specialises in snails. Back in the Plaza del Salvador the **Bar Alicantina** is famous for its seafood *tapas*.

Street corner on Plaza Nueva

If you visit only one museum in your trip make sure it's the **Museo de Bellas Artes** (Plaza del Museo; Tuesday–Friday 10am–2pm and 4–7pm, Saturday and Sunday 10am–2pm, closed Monday). For many decades it lay stranded in the unsalubrious streets bordering Seville's western railway station, Estación de Córdoba, and hardly helped its reputation by closing for years of interminable restoration. Work continues on the building – the old Convento de la Merced – but at least some of this great collection can now be visited. With the advent of Expo '92 and the closure of the railway station (which may become a Transport Museum), the area is set for rapid regeneration. In other words, take a taxi.

Inside you will find two thoroughly-restored rooms – and hopefully more by the time you read this. One is the main convent chapel with a baroque ceiling now so gloriously coloured it vies for attention with the great works below – a collection of religious paintings and sculptures gathered from the city's abundant and wealthy convents, monasteries and hospitals. The artists make an illustrious roll-call: El Greco, Pacheco, Velázquez, Cano, Zurbarán, Leal, Murillo... The adjoining room offers insights into not-so-old Seville – vistas of the Guadalquivir with steamships docked beside the Torre del Oro and Gonzalo Bilbao's tribute to the ladies of the Tobacco Factory, *Las Cigarerras*, painted as recently as 1915.

Two more museums are worth considering, both down on the Plaza de América at the southern end of the Parque de María Luisa. The **Museo de Artes y Costumbre Populares** (open Tuesday-–Saturday 10am–2pm, closed Sunday and Monday) is housed in the Mudéjar Pavilion left over from the Ibero-American Exposition. A haphazard assemblage of Sevillian costumes, bedrooms, portraits and agricultural odds-and-ends, it is nonetheless an enjoyable guide to the traditions and clichés of 19th and 20th century Andalusia.

Opposite this stands the **Museo Arqueológico** (open Tuesday–Sunday 10am–2pm, closed Monday), housed in the Renaissance Pavilion. The highlight is the Tartessian Carambolo Treasure discovered in 1958 in a field outside Seville. The collection covers Neolithic to Moorish times, including Roman mosaics and statues from Itálica and Ecija. Both these museums are free to EC members.

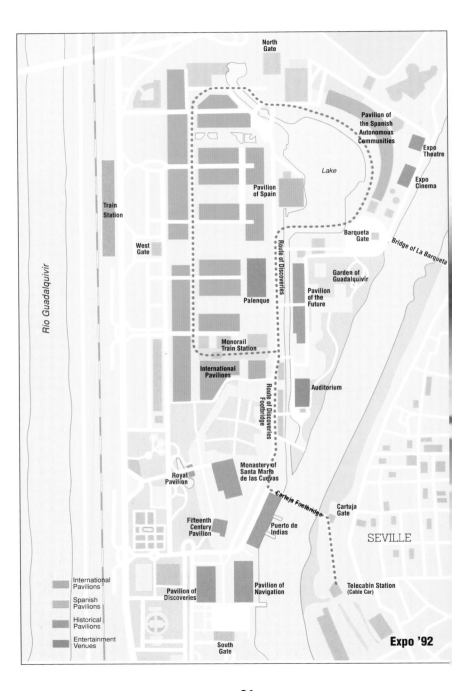

Expo '92

EXPO '92

'It will be a creative Exposition, representative of the collective universal drive towards innovation. It will bring alive the past 500 years and, in no uncertain terms, remind us that the second millenium of our era is just eight years away.' With these audacious words King Juan Carlos announced the selection of Seville as the host city for Expo '92 – a Universal Exposition that would celebrate the 500th anniversary of Christopher Columbus's discovery of America.

Soon afterwards Seville disappeared behind a jungle of scaffolding; 20,000 workers arrived from all parts of Spain and Portugal to descend on the Isla de la Cartuja, a 450-acre (215-ha) expanse of flat land to the west of the city that lies between the natural and artificial courses of the Guadalquivir. Since then they have been working flat out to construct a colossal theme park of pavilions and entertainment venues set in a planned landscape that includes 19 miles (30km) of roads, 22 miles (35km) of hedges and 350,000 trees and plants.

Such grand projects are nothing new to a city that started building the world's biggest Gothic cathedral in 1401. That same year

Monastery of Santa María de las Cuevas, focal point of Expo '92

Curro, Expo mascot

work had just begun on the Monastery of Santa María de las Cuevas, now the focal point of Expo '92. The monastery was used by Carthusian monks up until 1836 and is known today as 'La Cartuja'. It served as a refuge and place of burial for Columbus and his descendants and was later used as a military stronghold by the French during the Peninsular War.

In 1835 the Great Disentailment of religious buildings left it abandoned until 1841, when a Liverpudlian entrepreneur called Charles Pickman bought it as the site for Seville's famous ceramic factory, La Cartuja. Taking advantage of the area's abundant resources of clay he converted the monastery into a china factory, setting up furnaces in the cloister and a lathe shop in the church nave. At its peak it employed 1,200 workers producing a high quality English-style china. In 1982 the factory relocated.

This fortuitous heritage has allowed the Expo organisers neatly to link the discoveries of the Age of Columbus with the innovations of the Industrial Revolution. Universal Expositions traditionally endeavour to place mankind into a context of technological progress, a theme that dates from the first Great Exhibition held at London's Crystal Palace in 1851. Since then there have been 62 International or Universal Expositions – the most recent were Brus-

sels in 1958 ('A More Human World'), Montreal in 1967 ('Man and his World') and Osaka in 1970 ('Progress and Harmony of Mankind'), which attracted a record 60 million visitors. Expo '92 ('The Age of Discoveries') expects 20 million, half of whom will be from abroad.

Perhaps the most appealing aspect of Expo '92 is its desire to be far more than a Columbus-flavoured Disneyland. While there will be plenty of quincentennial celebration and entertainment it also has a strong commitment to being intellectually stimulating during its six-month run. The five central Pavilions along its 'Route of Discovery' aspire to plot the cultural and scientific advances of mankind as seen from a global perspective rather than our familiar Eurocentric or national viewpoints. With over 100 nations represented this is some challenge given the world's enduring taste for conflict and Spain's own disastrous colonisation of Latin America. Nevertheless the Expo message is resolute: let us enter the 21st century holding hands, for we are now part of a technology-shrunken, interdependent globe, united in our diversity by our common problems. As in the past, so in the future – Imagination and Science will see us through the world's problems. And if we could all do it via Seville, Andalusia and Spain so much the better....

Whether Expo '92 succeeds at this highbrow level remains to be seen. What is clear is that Seville doesn't intend to be left with a beautifully-tiled white elephant on its hands as it did after the Ibero-American Exposition of 1929. When Expo '92 closes its turnstiles the city will be bequeathed far more than a heap of unsold *Curros* (the chirpy, rainbow-beaked official mascot) and logo-embossed manhole covers. It will have a brand new transport network, 12 new hotels and a thoroughly tidied-up city. La Cartuja will become a science and technology park and Seville and Andalusia will once again be back on the world map.

Skeleton of one of the first Pavilions

Highlights

The theme of Expo '92 is 'The Age of Discoveries'. At its heart runs the 1.4 mile (2.3km) **Route of Discoveries** with five core Pavilions covering mankind's greatest achievements. At its southern end is the restored monastery of **La Cartuja** and the **Royal Pavilion**. Within the eastern part of the Cartuja complex is the introductory **Pavilion of the 15th Century**, built to resemble the Earth's sphere. This takes you back to the societies and cultures predominant in 1492 and includes a 15th-century courtyard garden, a 'time continuum' of Columbus's first voyage and an art exhibition 'World Art and Culture in 1492'. 'Cartuja 1400–1992' occupies the **monastery** itself and details the history of the building.

To the south of the Pavilion of the 15th Century is the **Pavilion of Discoveries** which retraces the great discoveries of the last five centuries. This has four strands: the great geographical discoveries of the 15th century; the great scientific discoveries of the 16–19th centuries; the Industrial Revolution; and the scientific and technological advances of the 20th century. Exhibition tools include an Omnimax 280° dome screen and a digital planetarium.

To the east of the Pavilion of Discoveries is the **Pavilion of Navigation**, next to the Port of the Indies and the Guadalquivir. This retraces the development of naval technology that made the great discoveries possible. The **Port of the Indies** recreates Seville's harbour at the height of the city's trade with the New World, including reconstructions of Columbus's three caravels and Magellan's *Nao Victoria*, the first ship to circumnavigate the world.

Further along the Route of Discoveries is the **Pavilion of the Future** displaying the latest technological advances and communications technologies. It has four sections: Energy, Communications, Environment and Space Exploration.

On the opposite side of the Route of Discoveries are the **International Pavilions**. These include the stands of the 111 nations taking part along with the 23 corporations and institutions attending – such as the United Nations, Red Cross, IBM, Siemens, Olivetti and Cruzcampo (who have built a whole brewery to quench the thirst of Expo '92). Most of the countries from Latin America are housed in the Plaza de América, one of the largest pavilions in Expo '92, while those from the EC line the Avenue of Europe. For the first

Pavilion of the 15th century

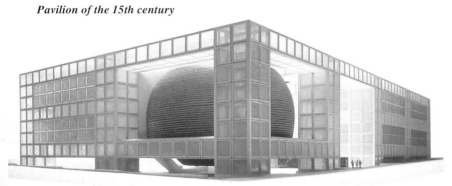

Model of the United Kingdom Pavilion

time in a Universal Exposition, Islamic countries are present. Look out for the **Japan Pavilion**, the largest wooden building ever constructed, and the **United Kingdom Pavilion**, designed by Nicholas Grimshaw with façades of water-walls. **Monaco's Pavilion** contains a walk-in aquarium while Switzerland's boasts a paper tower.

At the northern end of the Route of Discoveries stands the **Pavilion of Spain**, next to an artificial lake. Across the water in a long curve are 17 Pavilions representing each of Spain's Autonomous Regions. Look out for Navarre's, built like a traditional country house with a wood of tall beech trees inside.

The organisers of Expo '92 have given considerable thought to providing relief from the intense summer heat Seville experiences. Amongst its pergolas, fountains and waterfalls are 100 restaurants and 70 cafeterias and bars. The **Guadalquivir Garden** illustrates the history of gardening with an emphasis on Hispano-Arabic styles. Inside you will find the 301ft (92m) **Banesto Tower**, built a deferential metre lower than the Giralda, with a revolving cabin offering a bird's eye view over the site. This lies behind the Pavilion of the Future. Next to La Cartuja monastery you'll discover the **Garden of the Americas** with a collection of tropical plants introduced to Europe from that continent.

Entertainment

Expo '92 has 16 entertainment venues. These include the 6,200 seat **Cartuja Auditorium** where one of the largest stages in the world offers concerts and dance performances; the **Central Theatre**, staging international avant-garde and contemporary theatre, music and dance; the **Palenque**, an enormous tented area with concerts and performances of folk and 'roots' music; and the open air **Expo Cinema** which has a 1,500 seat capacity.

As well as these centrepiece venues there are lakeside shows, a Children's Theatre, street en-

Imitation caravel tying up at Expo

In the Maestranza bullring

tertainment and sporting events held at the Expo '92 athletics track. Every afternoon a cavalcade of performers and floats will pass along the Route of Discoveries and during the six months of Expo each participant will host its own **Special Day** of entertainment in the Palenque. As the Pavilions close at 10pm so **Expo Night** will begin, continuing until 4am with a fiesta of cafés, discotheques and street performances including a multimedia show of lasers, holograms and fireworks around the lake and dancing in the Palenque.

In Seville itself the new Teatro de La Maestranza is staging a programme of theatrical works which were originally inspired by the city while the 1920s Teatro de Lope de Vega puts on a series of purely Spanish plays. During July and August there will be an International Dance Festival staged in the Roman ampitheatre out at Itálica. In La Maestranza bullring horse shows and bullfights will take place (including the much-vaunted return from retirement of the legendary matador 'El Córdobes') with an exhibition every Saturday by the famous Royal School of Equestrian Art in Jerez entitled 'How the Andalusian Horses Dance'.

Part of the ritual of a bullfight

Getting There

Expo '92 has five entrance gates: **Barqueta Gate** – at the end of La Barqueta bridge; **Cartuja Gate** – at the start of La Cartuja footbridge; **North Gate, South Gate, West Gate** – next to the railway station (connections to Santa Justa Station and Madrid).

You can reach these gates by foot (La Cartuja footbridge) or by bus, car or taxi (other entrances). Parking facilities for 40,000 cars are available with a bus service to the entrance gates. There is also a cable-car that leaves from a telecabin station near La Cartuja Gate, capable of carrying 4,000 passengers per hour. For the duration of Expo '92 the Guadalquivir will be restored to its historic route through Seville (along the Canal de Alfonso XIII) allowing pleasure boats to land at the Puerto de Indias and give tours around the Isla de la Cartuja. Transport services to Expo '92 start at 7.30am and the exhibition's doors open at 9am. All Pavilions are open 10am–10pm. Once inside a continuous bus service and a 2-mile (3.1-km) elevated monorail helps visitors travel round the site.

Tickets and Information

Expo '92 runs from 20 April (Easter Monday) to 12 October (500th Anniversary of the Discovery of America).

Full-Day Tickets (valid 9am–4am), adults 4,000 ptas. Age 5–14, over 65, 1,500 ptas. **Evening Tickets** (valid 8.30pm–4am), all visitors 1,000 ptas.

Three-Day Passes (valid 9am–4am, consecutive days or not), all visitors 10,000 ptas.

Reduced Prices: available on 'Family Days' or for groups. Children under 5 enter free.

General Enquiries: Expo '92 Information Office, Plaza de Cuba 10. Tel: 462 87 00.

Hotel Reservations: CORAL, Recinto de la Cartuja, 41010 Sevilla. Tel: 429 00 92. Fax: 429 02 06.

For alternative accommodation (flats, private houses, halls of residences): Sevilla Abierta, EXHIBIT, Avenida República Argentina 37A, 41011 Sevilla. Tel: 428 49 36/26 36/46 26. Prior to the Exposition, Seville will be celebrating Semana Santa (12–19 April) and then its annual Feria (28 April–3 May).

Calendar of Events

Some of the many highlights of Expo '92 are listed below, but are of course subject to change. For a full advance programme of Cultural and Entertainment events write to: Expo '92, División de Actividades Culturales, Departamento Adjunto, Recinto de La Cartuja, 41010 Sevilla, Spain. Fax: (95) 429 06 34.

April

20 Opening Ceremonies and Inaugural Concerts.
21 Basque country Special Day. Peter Brook's *La Verbena de la Paloma* opens in the Lope de Vega theatre.
22 Catalonia Special Day.
22, 24, 26 Mozart's *Don Giovanni* at the Central Theatre.
23 Aragón Special Day. 24-hour Pop Gala at the Cartuja Auditorium.
24 Atlantic (record label) Gala at the Cartuja Auditorium.
24, 27, 30 Bizet's *Carmen* at the Teatro de La Maestranza.
27 First screening of silent film classic *Currito de la Cruz* with footage of Semana Santa in 1925 Seville.
27 April–31 May 'Passion' cycle of films in the Expo Cinema: legendary tales of love, passion and death from *Gone with the Wind* to *Paris, Texas*.

May

2 Madrid Special Day.
3 Bizet's *Carmen* at the Teatro de La Maestranza.
9 European Community Special Day.

8–13 Zarzuela Musical Spectacular at the Cartuja Auditorium (and various other dates through to August).
14–18 *Don Quixote* at the Lope de Vega Theatre.
17, 21, 25 Donizetti's *La Favorita* at the Teatro de La Maestranza, directed by Pavarotti.
21 United Kingdom Special Day.
21, 22, 23 Royal Ballet perform Britten's *The Prince of the Pagodas* and Prokofiev's *Romeo and Juliet* at the Cartuja Auditorium.
29 Castile-La Mancha Special Day.
TBA Lorca's *La Zapatera Prodigiosa* at the Lope de Vega Theatre.

June

1 Recital by Kiri Te Kanawa at the Teatro de La Maestranza.
6 Cruzcampo Special Day.
7 La Rioja Special Day.
9 Murcia Special Day.
11 Castile-León Special Day.
13 Navarre Special Day.
14 Extremadura Special Day.
17–19 Traditional Festivals of the Canary Islands.
26 United Nations Special Day.

All sorts of entertainment

Expo on stage

26–28 *Legend of Don Juan* (dance) at the Central Theatre.
26, 29 Verdi's *La Forza del Destino* at the Teatro de La Maestranza.
1–30 'Destiny' cycle of films in the Expo Cinema: heroic adventures and doomed heroes from *A Tale of Two Cities* to *Apocalypse Now*.
TBA Ingmar Bergman production at the Lope de Vega Theatre.

July

1, 2 Manuel de Falla's *El Sombrero de Tres Picos* (ballet) at the Cartuja Auditorium.
3 Balearic Islands Special Day. Royal National Theatre at the Lope de Vega Theatre.
3, 5, 7 Mozart's *The Marriage of Figaro* at the Teatro de La Maestranza.
4 *La Forza del Destino* at the Teatro de La Maestranza.
13 Jazz Week opens at the Cartuja Auditorium.
27 Galicia Special Day.
29 Series of New Music Concerts opens in the Cartuja Auditorium.
1–31 'Light' cycle of films in the Expo Cinema: masterpieces of cinematography from *Citizen Kane* to *Taxi Driver*.

August

2 Andalusia Special Day.
12 Cantabria Special Day.
5–6 *Sinking of the Titanic* (dance) at the Central Theatre.
1–31 'Illusion' cycle of films in the Expo Cinema: illusory gems from *My Fair Lady* to *Blade Runner*.

September

2 Recital by Luciano Pavarotti at the Cartuja Auditorium.
4, 6, 8 Mozart's *Don Giovanni* at the Teatro de La Maestranza.
9 Asturias Special Day.
14, 16, 18, 20 Rossini's *Il Barbieri di Siviglia* at Teatro de La Maestranza.
1 September–8 October 'Imagination' cycle of films in the Expo Cinema: from *Dracula* to *Star Wars*.
TBA Contemporary Spanish Theatre season at the Lope de Vega Theatre.

October

9 Valencia Special Day.
10 Motown Gala at the Cartuja Auditorium. Screening of *Currito de la Cruz* in the Expo Cinema.
12 Spain Special Day. Closing Galas.

Córdoba

Córdoba hugs a lazy bend of the Guadalquivir at the southern foot of the Sierra Morena, 87 miles (140km) east of Seville. For a city endowed with such a glorious past – it was the capital of Roman Spain and later of al-Andalus – it has become surprisingly small and provincial. The city's enduring attraction is the vast, innovative mosque constructed by the Moors on the north bank of the river between the 8th and 11th centuries: La Mezquita – one of the wonders of the world. The old quarters of Córdoba fan out around this magnet, a compact warren of whitewashed houses, winding alleys and flower-filled patios that generously reward the casual explorer. Beyond this sprawls the modern city where most of Córdoba's luxury hotels are located – but try if you can to stay in one of the several small hotels within the old quarter. If you haven't booked your accommodation ahead and can sacrifice comfort for character the area is well stocked with the cheaper *hostales* and *pensiones*, often with patios.

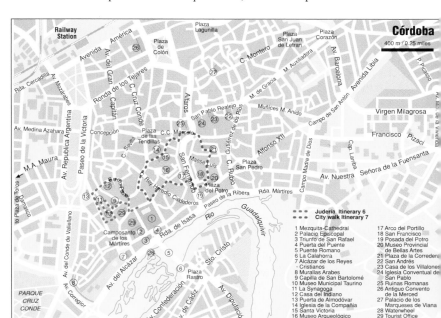

5. La Mezquita: A Guided Tour

La Mezquita is best visited in the early evening when the sun has warmed its ancient stones and the school groups and armed guards have disappeared. Spend the morning exploring the old quarter or visiting the Alcázar or Palacio de Viana (Itinerary 7).

If you enjoy architecture allow a good two hours for contemplating the mosque and bring a jacket – it's cool inside! Before you enter, consider calling into **El Caballo Rojo**, the most famous restaurant in Córdoba, to book a table for dinner (8.30pm–12am, ap-

Spend the morning in the Alcázar (above), before going into the Mezquita

proximately 11,000 pesetas for two; Cardenal Herrero 28, Tel: 47 43 42.) It specialises in *antigua cocina mozarabe*, traditional Córdoban dishes spiced and sweetened with Moorish flavours such as *cordero al miel* (lamb in honey) and *revuelto siglo XI* (scrambled egg *à la* 11th century).

Begin in the **Patio de los Naranjos**, which you can enter from either the east or west side of the Mezquita. Today it is an enclosed garden with bubbling fountains and lines of orange trees – an ideal place to sit and get your bearings. Construction of **La Mezquita** (10.30am–1.30pm, 4–7pm May–September; 3.30–5.30pm October–March) began in AD785, 21 years after Abd ar-Rahman I, founder of the Umayyad dynasty, declared himself Emir of al-Andalus. Until then Córdoba's Moorish and Christian communities had shared a Visigothic church that originally stood here, San Vicente, which had simply been partitioned into two parts. After purchasing the Christian half the Moors constructed a new mosque – making extensive use of materials from the old church – which occupied roughly a quarter of the space of what you see today.

Over the next two centuries, as Córdoba's wealth and prestige grew, successive rulers enlarged and embellished this original structure, extending the mosque east and as far south as the Guadalquivir

A Forest of Marble Palms

Palm trees, Arabian tents, Roman aqueducts, fans, acrobats on each other's shoulders . . . theories abound as to what inspired the Mezquita's architects to create the innovative pillar-and-arch design that makes Córdoba's mosque such a thrill. What is readily apparent is that they began with a pile of assorted columns and capitals gathered from the earlier Visigothic church and from other plundered sources around al-Andalus. The builders may also have kept one of the Visigothic church walls in place – a possible explanation for the Mezquita's great mystery: why does the *qibla*, the prayer wall traditionally facing east to Mecca, actually face south?

These columns, all of differing height and stone, were ingeniously incorporated into the building – sunk into the ground, raised up, inverted – and then topped by other columns. Two tiers of arches, constructed of red brick and white plaster, then bridged the gap between them – the higher arch supporting the roof, the lower strengthening the grid of columns. The result is apparently top-heavy, but when repeated row upon row, it creates a momentum and harmony that is ultimately spacious and agile. Later architects elaborated on this basic form by interlacing and poly-lobing (an effect resembling a bite-mark) the arches. The result, built more than a thousand years before the visual conundrums of Escher or computer graphics, is stone magic.

allowed. In 1236, when Ferdinand III captured Córdoba, the Mezquita reverted to Christian ownership: Catholic chapels were planted between its Roman and Visigothic pillars and many of its entrances blocked up. Over the course of the 16th century an extravagant cathedral was erected in its midst which earned a definitive rebuke from Charles V: 'You have built here something you could have built anywhere, but you have destroyed what was unique in the world.' This is rather ironic coming from an Emperor who made his own 'improvements' to the Alhambra and Seville's Alcázar and who himself sanctioned the work in the first place.

An appreciation of the Mezquita's former glory therefore requires some mental subtraction of Christian appendages. First remove all the filled-in arches along the mosque's northern wall, then open up all the closed doors in the walls surrounding the Patio; now lift off the 16th century bell-tower encasing the original minaret, swap the orange trees for olives, palms and cypresses and add a well and a waterwheel to the fountains.

In Arab cities a mosque is not a private religious compound but an integral part of the neighbouring streets – a combination of thoroughfare, meeting-place and, at the appointed hours, place of communal prayer. The Patio functioned as a courtyard for ritual ablution before prayer, the faithful being summoned by the wailing call from its slender minaret. Its main entrance would have been the **Puerta del Perdón** adjacent to this tower, which lies parallel to the principal entrance to the mosque, the Puerta de las Palmas (next to the four naves with wooden lattices). Both were redecorated in Mudéjar style but the latter is still flanked by two Roman columns and a plaque inscribed in Arabic stating, just like an architect's signboard, that Said ben-Ayub had been commissioned to build the mosque by Abd ar-Rahman in year 346 of the Muslim calendar.

Mezquita doorway

Today you enter the hall of the mosque through a small door on the south-east corner of the Patio, at which point this book becomes superfluous. If you want more information the itinerary resumes in the far corner to your right (by the wooden lattices), but have a wander first.

If you can find enough light to read this, you will hopefully be near to a lonely Visigothic font that by the end of the day is usually full of empty film boxes. This corner of the Mezquita is the old, original rectangle built by Abd ar-Rahman I. Along the walls, rows of Catholic chapels stretch into the gloom. Remove these and you can imagine how the serried pillars within the mosque were a continuation of the trees back in the Patio de los Naranjos, part of a subtle transition from the mundane to the divine that culminates in the *mihrab*, the sacred niche in the prayer wall where the Koran is kept.

Walking ahead (anti-clockwise) you will move into the first extension of the mosque, obvious from a slight rise in the floor, added by Abd ar-Rahman II in 833. To the left is the back of the cathedral *coro*. Further on is the vaulted ceiling of an aborted attempt to build a church here in the 15th century. To the left is the domed Capilla de Villaviciosa where the old mosque's *mihrab* would have been. Through a cut-away you can see the Capilla Real next door, redecorated in the 14th century in Mudéjar stucco, which would have been the *maqsura* or royal enclosure of the mosque.

Continuing on you enter the Mezquita's **major enlargement**, a legacy of the golden days of 10th century Córdoba. This was built in 964 by al-Hakam II, son of the self-proclaimed Caliph Abd ar-Rahman III. He pushed the southern wall right up to the river and built a new opulent *mihrab*, decorated with dazzling mosaics and a star-ribbed dome that was subsequently copied throughout Spain. This lies beyond a set of railings –

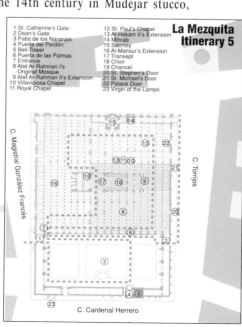

1 St. Catherine's Gate
2 Dean's Gate
3 Patio de los Naranjos
4 Puerta del Perdón
5 Bell-Tower
6 Puerta de las Palmas
7 Entrance
8 Abd Ar-Rahman I's Original Mosque
9 Abd Ar-Rahman II's Extension
10 Villaviciosa Chapel
11 Royal Chapel
12 St. Paul's Chapel
13 Al-Hakam II's Extension
14 Mihrab
15 Sacristy
16 Al-Mansur's Extension
17 Transept
18 Choir
19 Chancel
20 St. Stephen's Door
21 St. Michael's Door
22 Palace Door
23 Virgin of the Lamps

La Mezquita Itinerary 5

C. Magistral González Francés

C. Torrijos

C. Cardenal Herrero

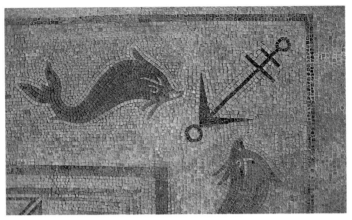

Moorish designs

the bejewelled side-chambers formed the *maqsura*. Now so far away from the Patio, domed sklights had to be introduced here.

Turning left you pass the cathedral sacristy and enter the **third extension** of the Mezquita, built by the belligerent al-Mansur in 990 to accommodate Córdoba's growing population. With the Alcázar to the west and the river to the south, his only option was to extend eastwards, widening both the hall and courtyard. Here the construction was conducted with more efficiency than artistry – the capitals of its uniform columns are less elaborate, the red is painted onto the arches – and probably reflects al-Mansur's greater interest in extending his caliphate, which reached as far as Santiago da Compostela.

Beside you stands the towering **Christian cathedral**, begun in 1523 and completed over the next two centuries. With its narrow aisles and lofty Capilla Mayor, designed to humble worshippers and direct their eyes to the heavens, it stands in marked contrast to the ubiquitous, unhierarchical Mezquita. It is nevertheless stunning, particularly the carved mahogany choir-stalls that fill the *coro* like some elaborate confection in dark chocolate.

Returning to the blinding light of the outside world, take the western exit from the Patio de los Naranjos and walk south towards the river. Here you will pass the richest of the Mezquita's

exterior façades. The first doorway you meet (St. Stephen's) was the original entrance to the Visigothic church and Abd ar-Rahman I's original mosque. Next you pass the extension by Abd ar-Rahman II and another door (St. Michael's) that would have been a royal passageway from the Alcázar to the mosque's *maqsura*.

Three more entrances follow, all with brass-faced doors. These all date from the al-Hakam II period – the centre one, with its Gothic arch stuck like a pointed hat on top of the earlier Moorish horseshoe neatly encapsulates the spirit of architectural one-upmanship that has created the Mezquita you see today. Everywhere historical interest is gained at beauty's expense – a truth borne out further when you reach the Mezquita's south-western corner. Here you will find an absurd collision of Time's left-overs – a Roman bridge, a 16th century triumphal gate built by Philip II and an 18th century monumental column to St Raphael. For much of the day these are strangled by an endless string of cars, horse-drawn carriages and tourist buses. Once the Mezquita closes, however, the city suddenly relaxes – a cathartic moment, and an ideal time to walk out across the Puente Romano. Pause beside the silty waters of the Guadalquivir and, like so many before you, contemplate Córdoba in the fading sunlight, before preparing yourself for dinner.

Horse-drawn carriages outside the Mezquita

6. Exploring the Judería

Córdoba's old Jewish quarter, the Judería, lies to the northwest of the Mezquita, and can be explored in a couple of hours.

A Sephardim community has been here since Roman times: subsequent persecution by the Visigoths forced its members to side with the invading Moors and as a reward for their support the Jews were allowed to remain in the city. For seven centuries they lived in fruitful co-existence with Córdoba's tolerant Muslim rulers until their expulsion by Ferdinand and Isabella in 1492.

The quarter is now an easy-going maze of narrow streets where craft shops and souvenir stalls are gradually infiltrating its smarter residences and neglected historic buildings. Start in the **Calle Cardenal Herrero** and walk west towards a T-junction of *souk*-like streets where you can pick up an ice cream at Helados Alberti to help keep your fellow pedestrians at bay. Take Calle Deanes (sharp right), past No 16 which has an above-average selection of the ubiquitous *filigrana de plata* (silver filigree) for which Córdoba has long been famous. Cassettes of flamenco and guitar music are another good buy around here.

At the end of the street turn left into Calle Buen Pastor which curls uphill to the Plaza Angel Torres. Nearby is the Casa del Indiano, a misleading title for a 15th century Mudéjar-style gate. Walk past this till you reach the more substantial **Almodóvar Gate**, part of the Moorish city walls. If you turn left beyond this (after bowing to the statue of Seneca), you can follow a pleasant, pool-lined promenade that runs beside the walls. At the end you'll meet a statue of the 12th century philosopher, medical writer and commentator on Aristotle, Averroës – one of the most famous thinkers of Córdoba's golden age. Near here an arch in the walls re-admits you to the Judería.

A sinuous alley (Calle La Luna) leads to a crossroads where you turn left (Calle Tomas Conde) into the Plazuela Maimónides. Here the **Museo Municipal de Arte Taurino** (9.30am–1.30 pm, 5–8pm; 4–7pm in winter; closed Monday) is dedicated to the art of bullfighting. Continue past a statue of Maimónides, a 12th-century Jewish scholar and philosopher whose treatises on medicine were translated throughout medieval Europe. To your right you will find the **Zoco**, a handicrafts market with studios and workshops selling high-quality Córdoban leather goods, jewellery and ceramics. Further on (Calle Judios) you'll encounter one of Spain's three surviving **synagogues** (the other two are in Toledo). It is remarkable that this small, intimate place of worship still exists: it dates from 1314 and has walls bearing Mudéjar ornament and Hebraic inscription. Over the centuries it has served as a hospital for rabies victims, hermitage, cobbler's, school and warehouse before being rescued (open 10am–2pm, 3.30–5.30pm, 10am–1.30pm Sunday, closed Monday.)

After the synagogue turn right into Calle Averroës which will take you round the back of the Zoco, past the beautifully dilapidated church of San Bartolomé and (left at No 5) into the Plaza del Cardenal Salazar. Here the busy restaurant **El Churrasco** specialises in grilled meats (*churrasco* is a grilled pork dish with pepper sauce) and has a good selection of *tapas* (Calle Romero 16, Tel: 29 08 19). From here Calle Romero will take you back to the Mezquita. **Taberna Pepe** at the bottom, despite its hectic location, is a friendly bar and restaurant, good for a quick coffee or a slow lunch. If you want to escape the tour groups try **La Fragua**, up an alley at the bottom of Calle Tomas Conde.

7. City Walk and Museums

This half-day itinerary takes you to the less-visited eastern part of Córdoba where the old city intermingles with the new. Venture out in the morning if you like markets and shopping, in the afternoon if you enjoy the peace of empty streets.

Start in **Calle Cardenal Herrero** and walk east to its junction with Calle Magistral González Francés, where you can walk up the narrow Calle Encarnación. **Taller Meryan** at No 12 is a workshop with a typical range of traditional Córdoban tooled and embossed leather goods for sale. A quintessential part of Córdoba's character which you will encounter frequently in this walk is the patio. These inner courtyards were built by the Moors as cool central sanctuaries where their owners could escape the fierce heat of the summer. They often have a central fountain encircled by ferns with the surrounding walls bedecked with brightly-flowering pot-plants, patterned ceramic plates and cheerful *azulejos*.

Turn right, then left by the Hostal La Milagrosa (Calle Horno del Cristo) into the **Plaza del Jerónimo Páez**. This contains a statue of Lucan and the province's Museo Arqueólogico, housed in a Renaissance palace, which is, alas, closed for restoration. Take the pedestrian Calle Julio Romero de Torres which winds round (past No 19) to descend the Calle del Portillo. At the bottom an ancient archway takes you beyond the old city walls – opposite is the Baroque Convento de San Francisco. Cross the road and turn right then second left to pass the Hostal Maestre (Calle Romero Barros), which delivers you into the charming **Plaza del Potro**.

The plaza, which has a rare view out to the cornfields south of Córdoba, gets its name from the *potro* (foal) soaring above its gushing 16th century fountain. A plaque nearby immodestly reminds visitors that Cervantes mentioned the square 'en la mejor novela de mundo'. *Don Quixote*'s creator stayed in its *pousada* (inn), now an arts centre which contains a permanent exhibition (free entry) of *guadamecí* – a style of embossed and coloured leatherwork introduced to Córdoba from North Africa in the 9th century.

Opposite is the **Museo Provincial de Bellas Artes** (May-September 6–8pm; October–April 10am–2pm, 5–7pm; closed Monday), housed in the former Hospital de la Caridad. It contains an agreeable miscellany of Córdoban *objets trouvés* including Roman relics, religious portraits, prints of old Córdoba, one Goya engraving, some 20th century sculpture. Next door is the **Museo Julio Romero de Torres**, devoted to a local painter (1880–1930) responsible for

Córdoban patio

the sultry and (to male Spanish eyes) erotic portraits of underdressed Andalusian women.

At the top of the Plaza del Potro, a small street (past No 15) takes you past a puppeteers' workshop and round into Calle Armas. Head straight on via Calle Sanchez Peña to reach the large rectangular **Plaza de la Corredera**. A traditional site for the city's markets, bullfights and entertainments, the galleried brick buildings enclosing the square were built in 1688. Today it is the scene of an easy-going market. Leave by the top left corner – if you are ready for a drink and some *raciones* turn left just before the top of the hill where the quiet **Taberna Salinas** (Tundidores 3) specialises in *cocina tradicional cordobesa* – try some Córdoban *salmorejo* (cold soup) or excellent *berenjenas fritas* (fried aubergines).

Further on you will see the restored columns of a Roman temple standing somewhat bizarrely next to the modern Ayuntamiento. If you intend to visit the **Palacio de los Marqueses de Viana** (June–

Puppeteers' workshop by Plaza del Potro

September and Sunday 9am–2pm; October–May 10am–1pm, 4–
6pm; closed Wednesday and 1st week of June), turn right here. This
is a 16th-century Córdoban stately home in private ownership until 1980. With no fewer than 13 patios and 38 rooms and galleries
crammed with antiques from all over the world it is guaranteed to
trigger the imagination. Whirlwind guided tours only.

Back on the walk, continue uphill along Calle Claudio Marcelo.
This culminates in Córdoba's bus-clogged central square, the **Plaza
de las Tendillas**, but you will find life quieter if you turn left by
the Ferreteria Central – which does a good line in hand-made calf-
skin working boots – into a pedestrianised shopping precinct (Calle
Conde de Cárdenas).

Walking through you will discover the 16th century Jesuit
church **Salvador y Santo Domingo**, a monument to St Raphael (a
civic obsession) and further ahead the curved
façade of the 18th century **Iglesia de Santa
Victoria**. Skirting this to the violin strains
that often emanate from the Music Conserva-
tory in Calle Juna Valera, you reach a main
street (Calle Blanco Belmonte) where you
turn left to head downhill towards the Mezquita. There is a good view of its tower from
the Plaza Buenavento. Take a small alley to
the left of this plaza (past No 2) which
will lead you to Calle Velazquez Bosco.
This runs down to the Mezquita: on
the way take a trip up the **Callejón
de las Flores**, the vainest, most-pho-
tographed street in Córdoba.

Plaza del Potro

GRANADA

Only 50 miles (80km) from the Mediterranean coast, Granada stands a cool 2,247ft (685m) above sea level. Once stacked up around three foothills of the **Sierra Nevada** – Albaicín, Sacromonte and Alhambra – the city now oozes out over the eastern end of the *vega*, the long fertile plain which in Moorish times was a vast market garden full of orchards, farms and watermills. Further east rise the mountains of the Sierra Nevada, their snowy peaks providing the waters for the two principal rivers that weave through the city, the Darro and the Genil.

Granada's famous Alhambra can absorb as much of your time as you care to give it. Spare a few hours for exploring the cobbled streets of the Albaicín too: once a separate walled Moorish city, it has yet to succumb to the prettification that similar old quarters in Seville and Córdoba have undergone. Modern-day Granada, as you will discover unless you are fortunate enough to be staying in the ethereal surroundings of the Alhambra hill, is hectic, polluted and relentlessly persecuted by traffic. However, it has a lively university and a good programme of cultural activities.

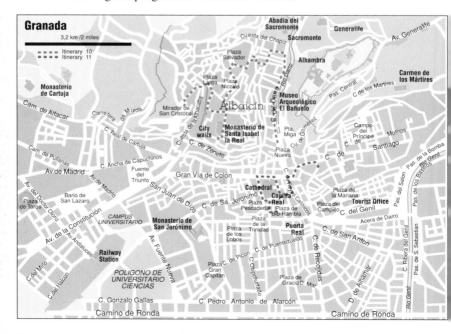

8. Alhambra I: Alcazaba and Generalife

I suggest that you make the most of your two-day entry ticket to the Alhambra by taking it gently and visiting different areas on different days.

The traditional approach to the Alhambra involves a steep, half-hour walk up from the Plaza Nueva, so award yourself a good breakfast. The ascent soon discards the grimy shops of the Cuesta de Gomérez in favour of the cool woods of the Alhambra hill, passing through the **Puerta de las Granadas** (Gate of the Pomegranates – the city's emblem) and (take the left hand path) delivering you outside the citadel's most imposing entrance, the **Torre de la Justicia**. As you wind through this great Moorish gateway two symbols above its horseshoe arches remind visitors that they are entering the world of Islam: a hand (representing the faith's five tenets: the oneness of God, prayer, fasting, alms-giving and pilgrimage) and a key (rep-

Puerta de las Granadas

resenting the power Allah gave the Prophet to open and close the gates of heaven).

Beyond this gate some steps lead to a reminder that you are also entering the world of mass tourism: the main ticket office. If you prefer to arrive by taxi or by bus (No 2 from the Plaza Isabel la Católico), just follow the signs here. Whatever way you come, you'll inevitably confront the massive bulk of **Charles V's** decidedly un-Moorish **palace**, commissioned in 1526 but built almost a century later. Visit it first, for its stark and haughty Renaissance grandeur contrasts informatively with the frenzied eggbox ceilings and crazy-stuccoing you will encounter later in the Nasrid Palaces. The design – by Pedro Mach-

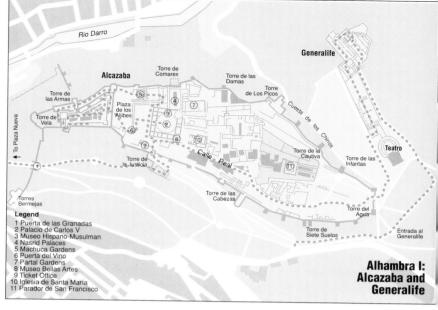

**Alhambra I:
Alcazaba and
Generalife**

Legend
1 Puerta de las Granadas
2 Palacio de Carlos V
3 Museo Hispano-Musulman
4 Nasrid Palaces
5 Machuca Gardens
6 Puerta del Vino
7 Partal Gardens
8 Museo Bellas Artes
9 Ticket Office
10 Iglesia de Santa Maria
11 Parador de San Francisco

uca – is a masterpiece and sadly his only surviving work. Once within its inner courtyard you will immediately appreciate the simplicity and power of the architect's concept – a circle in a square, executed in unadorned stonework. The courtyard, once used for fairs and bullfights, was to have been eventually covered over but thankfully this never happened.

To the left of the courtyard is the **Museo Hispano-Musulman** (10am–2pm, closed Monday). It is worth visiting, if only to see the famous Jarrón de la Alhambra, a 14th century Nasrid vase decorated with gazelles and as good a definition of beauty as any. The

The Alhambra's Court of the Myrtles

collection contains many relics from the Alhambra's glory days: ceramics, *azulejos*, pottery lamps, carved roof-beams, marquetry chessboards, even a copper minaret – all of which will help you bring this great Moorish stage set to life. Opposite the museum's exit is the **Museo Bellas Artes** (10am–2pm, closed Monday): if you push on through its worthy collection of religious paintings and sculpture you'll find the 19th century galleries have an entertaining display of coy and picaresque characters from Romantic Andalusia.

After collecting some almonds or hazelnuts from the sweet-seller back by the ticket office, continue through the **Puerta del Vino** towards the battlements of the Alcazaba. This is the oldest part of the fortress – some sections date from the 9th century but the two towers overlooking the Plaza de los Aljibes (Cisterns) are 13th century. Their burnt red walls (*al-Hamra* is Arabic for 'the red') remind us that the Alhambra began life as a military garrison. The plaza you are crossing was once the moat, then an underground cistern, and now, appropriately, contains a kiosk selling beer and soft drinks.

You enter the **Alcazaba** by the Torre Quebrada (Broken Tower) and pass around the the Torre del Homenaje (Homage Tower) to reach the Plaza de Armas – which would have once been filled with houses and barracks. Today only the dungeons and cisterns are visible. On its far side signs guide you towards the main tower, the **Torre de Vela** (Watchtower). On the way be sure to enjoy the lit-

The Tale of the Alhambra

Construction of the Alhambra began in 1238 at the behest of Ibn-al-Ahmar, founder of the Nasrid dynasty. He rebuilt the ancient fortress of the Alcazaba, originally separated from the main hill by a ravine (now the Plaza de los Aljibes) and diverted the waters of the Darro to supply the new citadel. Most of the palatial splendour you see today was built in the 14th century by craftsmen who fled here as al-Andalus shrivelled with the Reconquest.

The Catholic Monarchs Ferdinand and Isabella admired the palaces and even restored parts of them. They installed a cathedral within the mosque (replaced in the late 16th century by the Iglesia de Santa María) and built the Franciscan convent (now the Parador). Their grandson Charles V was more heavy-handed, demolishing more than he replaced and plonking his imperial palace down on the site of the cemetery. With the expulsion of the Moors, along with some minor earthquakes and a gunpowder explosion in 1590, the Alhambra fell into decline.

Some two centuries later the Alhambra was ransacked by Napoleon's troops. This parlous state of decay ultimately proved beneficial, for it endeared the Alhambra to the Romantic writers, artists and travellers then discovering (some would say inventing) the exotic Spain of the 19th century. 'The Alhambra,' Benjamin Disraeli declared in 1830, 'is the most imaginative, the most delicate and fantastic creation that ever sprang up on a Summer night in a fairy tale.' Such eulogistic appreciation of this clapped-out castle goes a long way to explaining why we are all gathered here today.

By 1870 the Alhambra had been declared a national monument. Today it is visited by over 1.5 million people a year. Your gratitude to the Romantics who rediscovered it should be expressed by purchasing a copy of *Tales of the Alhambra* (on sale everywhere), written by an American diplomat, Washington Irving, who lived here for a few months in 1829, and by doing a bit of dreaming yourself.

Visiting the Alhambra

Every day some 4,000 people visit the Alhambra. Admission tickets have three parts, allowing you to visit the Alcazaba, Nasrid Palaces and the Generalife in any order; all are open Monday–Saturday 9am–8pm, Sunday 9am–5.45pm (in winter, 4 April–25 September, 9.30am –6pm daily). On Sunday entrance is free after 3pm, but the Palacio Carlos V and Comares Baths are closed.

Tickets are valid for two days, so accept this invitation to linger in paradise. A complete tour involves walking almost 2 miles (3.2km), but this is a vast walled garden filled with historical delights and should not be hurried through. You should come equipped for indolence: take a book big enough to snooze under and a stack of unwritten postcards, perhaps a sketchpad or a notebook, certainly a lover and a bag of cherries.

If you are fortunate enough to be in Granada on a Tuesday, Thursday or Saturday (in winter Saturday only), pay a visit to the Nasrid Palaces at night, open 10–12pm. At such times the Alhambra's magic becomes palpable: liberated from the herds of video-headed tour groups that rampage by day, its pools and patios lapse into a shadowy, moonlit peace underscored by distant footfalls and fountains. It's worth changing your travel plans to include such a nocturnal visit. Just hail a taxi and say the magic word 'Alhambra.'

tle-visited Jardín de los Adarves with its classic terrace view of the Sierra Nevada. There are yet better views to be enjoyed from the top of the Torre de Vela: for centuries its bell was used to tell the farmers of the *vega* when to irrigate their crops.

The Alhambra's one-way system directs you next down beside the battlements and out to the Machuca Gardens. The entrance to the **Nasrid Palaces** follows, but I suggest you let them wait till tomorrow, or at least until after lunch. Instead make your way back to the Charles V palace and around into the centre of the Alhambra precinct. Here the Calle Real leads up past the Iglesia de Santa María to the **Restaurante Polinario**, which has a monopoly on catering to hungry Alhambra-goers but which nonetheless offers a satisfying buffet for a reasonable price. Further on is the luxury **Parador de San Francisco** (with restaurant), converted from a convent dating from 1495.

To the right of the Parador is the entrance to the **Generalife**, approached along a promenade of cypresses. This was the Nasrid rulers' summer residence, created in the mid-13th century and re-created today as a horticultural paradise inspired by Moorish themes. The gardens incorporate features similar to those you will find in the palace buildings – hidden entrances, enclosed gardens, pools and fountains – only here their intention is the creation of delight. Towards the end of the Generalife are some restored pavilions with views to Sacromonte hill. Above are more terraces and a romantic water staircase. To leave, an avenue of oleanders nearby leads to the eastern exit. From here you can drift back down through the verdant Alamedas (beech avenues) to Granada.

View from the Alcazaba

9. Alhambra II: Nasrid Palaces and Gardens

The Nasrid Palaces are a tourist honey-pot: if you can wait until 2pm or later, when most of the tour groups are hopefully at lunch, they should be less crowded. Beyond the palaces lie some idyllic gardens and patios, so plan to spend the afternoon here.

The entrance lies to the far side of the Palacio de Carlos V. The first room you enter is the Mexuar, an audience chamber used for judicial and administrative business. In the 18th century it was converted into a chapel – the *azulejos* are from Seville, and in Moorish times there would have been a cupola and lantern rather than the present carved wood roof. At the end is the Oratory, from which there is the first of many views out over the Albaicín and Sacromonte hills.

Another reception area follows, the Golden Room, decorated in Mudéjar style after the Reconquest. Opposite it is the Mexuar Patio (which would make an excellent squash court), and the façade of the Comares Palace. Here you can study the intricate patterns of the plasterwork, constructed in low relief to catch the sunlight, that was used to decorate many of the palaces' walls. Islam proscribes the depiction of the human form and the Alhambra's craftsmen vigorously pursue the abstract: the intention is to direct the eye to the infinite and the mind to the divine by a rhythmic dazzle of repeated floral shapes, interlocking geometric forms, multi-centred grids and ribbons of Koranic inscription joined together to proclaim the oneness of God.

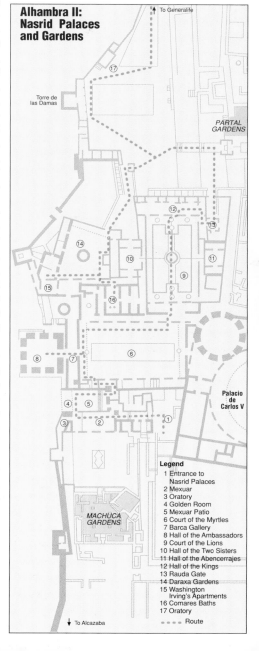

Alhambra II: Nasrid Palaces and Gardens

To Generalife

Torre de las Damas

PARTAL GARDENS

Palacio de Carlos V

MACHUCA GARDENS

To Alcazaba

Legend
1 Entrance to Nasrid Palaces
2 Mexuar
3 Oratory
4 Golden Room
5 Mexuar Patio
6 Court of the Myrtles
7 Barca Gallery
8 Hall of the Ambassadors
9 Court of the Lions
10 Hall of the Two Sisters
11 Hall of the Abencerrajes
12 Hall of the Kings
13 Rauda Gate
14 Daraxa Gardens
15 Washington Irving's Apartments
16 Comares Baths
17 Oratory
- - - - Route

The Partal Gardens

Once you take the small passage leading into the **Court of the Myrtles** two further principles followed by the Alhambra's architects become apparent: the desire to create awe-inspiring histrionic effects (with bland exteriors and concealed entrances for example), and the concern to make natural elements, particularly light and water, an integral and active part of the architecture. Now you are in the Serallo, the heart of the royal palace where foreign emissaries would have been received. As you skirt the long goldfish pond (clockwise) you pass a small niche that allows close inspection of the stalactital stuccowork. The faded colours still caught in its recesses remind us that such ornamentation, only made from a crude assemblage of brick, wood and plaster, was once painted and gilded.

Next you pass through the Barca Gallery, an ante-chamber to the splendid **Hall of the Ambassadors** where the Moorish Kings presided. Be sure to take a seat here so you can contemplate its impressive domed ceiling, a celestial cosmos of inlaid wood depicting the seven heavens revolving around the seat of God.

Continue around the Court of the Myrtles and through a small passage leading into the *harem*, the private section of the palace and also the last to be built. It is heralded by the famous **Court of**

Stuccowork in the Nasrid Palaces

the Lions, which some feel to be the decadent swansong of a doomed monarchy. The design represents a symbolic Islamic paradise: an enclosed garden (substitute plants for what is now gravel) with a central fountain from which the four rivers of paradise flow into four restful pavilions surrounded by a forest of marble palms. Around the fountain stand 12 lions, perhaps representing the 12 signs of the zodiac or the tribes of Israel.

Here, and in the adjacent four rooms, the Sultan and his entourage resided: to the left as you enter are his wife's apartments (Hall of the Two Sisters) with a cupola said to have over 5,000 cavities. Opposite this is the Hall of the Abencerrajes, used for entertainments, with an octagonal ceiling resembling the rear-view of a just-launched rocket. Ahead is the King's Hall with alcoves behind that were once bedchambers. The ceilings above these are leather and painted with scenes of courtly life, presumably executed by a Christian artist under Moorish commission.

The exit from the palaces leads through the ivy-clad **Rauda Gate** into the Partal Gardens (formerly the servant's quarters and vegetable plots), where a kiosk nearby offers the welcome chance for a cool drink. Later you can wander down the terraces and left to the Lindaraja and Daxara Gardens, both former apartments of the harem that were remodelled in the 16th century. It was in this secluded corner of the Alhambra that Washington Irving lived in 'delicious thraldom' while he wrote his bestseller. Here you will also discover the damp, tiled chambers and star-spangled domed roofs of the **Baño de Comares**, the Royal Baths – the most intimate and evocative part of the whole complex.

Returning to the Partal Gardens you will pass a pavilion built above the fortress walls (Torre de las Damas) and faced by a large pool guarded by two lions said to have been rescued from the lunatic asylum that occupied part of the Alhambra in the mid-19th century. Nearby is a small Moorish oratory while further on a string of ancient towers and modern gardens lead you up towards the Generalife.

Into the gardens

10. Exploring the Albaicín

Piled up on a steep hill facing the Alhambra, the Albaicín was the heart of Moorish Granada and seat of the royal court for two centuries before the Nasrids built their palaces on the opposite side of the Darro river. When the city fell to Ferdinand and Isabella in 1492 the Albaicín had 60,000 inhabitants; by the start of the 17th century the ensuing persecution and expulsion of the rebellious 'moriscos' (Muslim converts) reduced this to 6,000.

Traditionally a poor quarter, the Albaicín is now a pleasant, unpretentious maze of narrow streets lined with whitewashed houses, high-walled palaces and neglected churches and convents. Despite the gentrification seeping through the alleys, its Moorish character persists, the air still delicately perfumed with jasmine and mule dung. Head up here around midday for a late lunch and stroll: you can climb up from the **Plaza Nueva** (a long slog) but it is wiser to take a taxi or a No 12 bus (from Calle Acera de Darro, near to Galerías Preciados) up to the **Mirador de San Cristóbal**.

From this Mirador there is a fine view over Granada and the *vega*: in the foreground you will see the old city walls of the Albaicín. From here you can take Calle Brujones (to the left of a souvenir shop) and turn right to descend a steep cobbled street (Cuesta de San Cristóbal). Immediately you will pass two recurring features of the Albaicín: to the left an *aljibe* (water cistern), to the right a *cármen* or private walled house and garden.

Drop down the hill into the Plaza Almona, then go left up into the **Plaza Larga**. This is the hub of the Albaicín – in the morning a market, for the rest of the day an open-air café and meeting place. In the right-hand corner of the plaza stands the 11th century Puerta Nueva with a defensive dog-leg passage – turn right here (Callejón de las Minas) to reach a small park, Placeta del Cristo de las Azucenas. This adjoins two of the Albaicín's best-known buildings (both currently closed for restoration) – the **Monastery of Santa Isabel la Real** (1501) and behind it another Moorish palace, the **Dar al-Horra**. If you continue down Calle Pilar Seco and turn right past the monastery you will reach the quiet **Plaza San Miguel Bajo**, a good place to stop for a drink or light lunch – Bar Lara offers meats from the Alpujarras.

Aljibe in the Albaicín

Plaza San Miguel Bajo

Walk back to the park and continue straight ahead, along the Camino Nuevo de San Nicolás, where a curve to the left will lead you up some steps to the Mirador de San Nicolás and a postcard-perfect view of the Alhambra silhouetted against the Sierra Nevada. Ahead you can see the old city walls running across Sacromonte hill, along with the abandoned caves of Granada's old gypsy quarter. Descend the steps and turn right to reach a small plaza beside the Iglesia del Salvador.

From here you can zig-zag your way downhill by any route that keeps you facing the Alhambra. Following the signs to the **Cármen-Restaurante Mirador de Morayma** (1.30–3.30pm, 8.30–11.30pm, closed Sunday night, Tel: 22 82 90) is a good option, leading you to one of Granada's most delightful restaurants: not only does it offer the rare chance to get inside a flower-filled *cármen*, it also serves local specialities like *espinacas al Sacromonte* and *habas con jámon*, along with convent-made sweets and Sierra Nevada cheeses. An easy route down from here is via Calle Placeta de Toqueros, where you turn left then right to descend the gentle gradient of the Cuesta de la Victoria. Now you are beside the Darro ravine. The plaza here has a gentle neighbourhood atmosphere – worth returning to in the evening when it becomes an endearing mix of café-dawdlers, basketball-players and baked potato-sellers. A range of bars along the **Paseo del Padre Manjón** serve *tapas* and small dishes – La Fuente plays good Spanish pop music.

From here you can follow the Darro back towards the city centre along a narrow, traffic-constipated street that gives a clue to what Granada must have been like. On the way you will pass the Casa del Castril, home of the **Museo Arqueológico** (Tuesday–Saturday 10am–2pm), and nearby **El Bañuelo** (No 31, knock on the door; Tuesday–Friday 10am–2pm, 4–6pm; Saturday and Sunday morning only) which houses some very well-preserved 11th-century Arab public baths with domed roofs and star-shaped vents.

Beside the river Darro

11. Morning Walk in the Cathedral Quarter

You could quite easily pass through Granada without even noticing it had a cathedral. Lost in a huddle of nondescript buildings below the Gran Vía de Colón, it is built on the site of the city's main mosque, a Christian spaceship rocketed into the heart of Muslim Granada. The surrounding district bears witness to this mixed heritage, a patchwork of pedestrian shopping streets and leafy plazas that is liveliest in the mornings.

Tombs of Ferdinand and Isabella in the Capilla Real

The **Plaza de Bib-Rambla**, just west of Calle Reyes Católicos, is a pleasant starting point. Once the site of a great Moorish gate, its pavement cafés are a good spot to sit and watch Granada wake up. Close to these cafés Calle Pescadería will lead you into Granada's central market area, a sprawl of stalls that adjoin the covered **Mercado Municipal de San Agustin**.

From the centre of Calle Pescadería the short Calle Marquesa de Gerona, a street devoted to knife-sellers, will take you to the Plaza de las Pasiegias. After several false starts, construction of Granada's **cathedral** (daily 10.30am–1pm, 4–7pm) began in 1523 and employed a procession of famous artists: here you see its main façade, designed in 1667 by Alonso Cano. Skirt left around the building, past two portals that are the work of the cathedral's principal architect, Diego de Siloé, and along Gran Vía de Colón until you discover the entrance, inevitably mobbed by carnation-sellers.

The **interior** of the cathedral, which was not completed until 1714, is cavernous and frigid. A *retablo* dedicated to Saint James (left as you enter) clamours for attention, as does Siloé's domed Capilla Mayor – half way up its central arch are two statues of Ferdinand and Isabella kneeling in prayer. Curiously the small **mu-**

Lead coffins in the crypt

seum (at the opposite end) and the intimate **sacristy** (right as you enter) are of more interest: the first contains a giant monstrance paraded through the streets at Corpus Christi, the second some elegant Parisian chests-of-drawers and a friendly Ellicot 'Strike Silent' grandfather clock.

When you leave the cathedral turn right into Calle Oficios, where you can visit the **Capilla Real** (daily 10.30am–1pm, 4–7pm), resting place of Ferdinand and Isabella. Once again the side-shows prove the best attractions: first you encounter the sacristy (the usual point of entry, via the Lonja, is closed for restoration), rich with regal art and treasures. Push on through to the chapel itself, where the marble tombstones (1517) of Ferdinand and Isabella (nearest as you enter, their actual remains in the crypt below) are upstaged by the larger ones of Philip the Fair and Joan the Mad, placed there by their son, Charles V. The chancel is fronted by a magnificent wrought-iron grille, and nearby hangs a triptych by Dierick Bouts. You'll find more Flemish masters in the sacristy, including works by Memling, van der Weyden and Botticelli.

Back in Calle Oficios you'll pass the site of Granada's Arab university, **La Madraza**, founded in 1349 by Yussuf I and now part of Granada University – if the door is open you can inspect a small, richly-decorated oratory across the patio, only uncovered in 1893. Carrying on down the street and left through a small arch, you will enter the Alcaicería, a 19th century reconstruction of the Arab silk market that originally stood here. Today it is a repetitive parade of souvenir stalls. If you continue straight on you can cross Calle Zacatin, a long pedestrian shopping street, to reach Calle Reyes Católicos. Directly across the road in Calle Lopez Rubio you will see (if the traffic lets you) a horseshoe arch marking the entrance to the **Corral del Carbón**. This was once a 14th century caravanserai where merchants and their animals were quartered. Inside is a central courtyard surrounded by three-storeyed galleries: one corner houses a branch of Artespaña, a state-run handicrafts shop.

If you are ready for lunch, go up Calle Reyes Católico to the **Plaza Isabel la Católico**, dominated by a statue (pictured left) commemorating this queen's support for Columbus. From here you can take Calle Pavaneras to the small, tree-shaded, car-cluttered **Plaza Padre Suarez**, where **Seis Peniques** offers a range of set menus in an alfresco setting opposite the Casa de los Tiros, an early 16th century mansion – note the muskets peeping from the upper windows. For a classier venue with expensive but exquisite cuisine, try the cellar-restaurant at the bottom of this plaza, **Alacena de Las Monjas** (Tel: 22 40 28).

65

What to Buy

If the souvenir-sellers had their way we'd all return with suitcases full of gypsy costumes, children's flamenco dresses, personalised bullfighting posters, castanets, mantillas, Giralda pencil sharpeners, Mezquita wine-flasks and Alhambra table-lamps. Don't let such mass-produced memories of Andalusia obscure the fact that you can also buy quality versions of these clichés: broad-brimmed hats, fans, hand-made shawls, guitars and wrought ironwork (*esparta*) are also sold in specialist shops.

Leather goods, jewellery and ceramics are widely sold – keep an eye out for shoes and sandals, silver filigree, decorative plates and bowls, *azulejos* and kitchenware – all particularly good value. In recent years the quality of handicraft products has improved, with good modern designs of hats, T-shirts, jewellery and stationery now available. Cheap belts, wallets, bags and baskets can be bought from African hawkers who will barter; look out too for the bargain shops with signs saying *Todo a 100 pesetas* – great fun.

Flamenco dresses

If you're searching for locally made presents consider sherry, convent-made sweets, virgin olive oil, cassettes of guitar music, figs, honey, almonds and saffron. Other favourite Spanish purchases are *cava* (champagne – try the Delapierre or Freixenet labels), cigars from the Canary Islands or Cuba, carved olive wood utensils, terracotta kitchenware, *paella* dishes, candle-holders, *sangría* jugs, Lladró porcelain, *alfombras* (carpets and floor-rugs) and *jarapas* (multicoloured rugs and car-seat covers made from cotton strips). In the department stores, shoes, children's clothes, swimwear, towels and stationery are worth investigating.

Seville

Seville's main shopping street is the serpentine **Calle Sierpes**. At its southern end you'll find Seville's high fashion designers Victorio and Lucchino (No 87) while further up Martian (No 74) offers a pleasing display of Sevillian ceramics and pottery. Zadi (No 48) has a serious collection of fans, mantillas and Lladró while the old-fashioned Maquedano (No 40) stocks a classic range of Andalusian hats. In a side street Europa Rapto (Calle Rivero 5) has innovative designer clothes. To the east the Plaza de Jesús de la Passion is the city's matrimony corner with several jewellery shops, while to the west Iñiguez – La Casa de las Alfombras (corner of Calle O'Donnell and Calle Velázquez) has a good range of *jarapas*. Sevilla Rock, opposite El Corte Inglés (Plaza del Duque de la Victoria) sells Spanish pop and guitar music including flamenco and *sevillanas*. Nearby in the Plaza de la Concordia (No 2) is a branch of the state-run up-market handicrafts shop, Artespaña.

Cerámica Santa Ana

For ceramics La Alacena (Calle Alfonso XII 25) has top-of-the-range china and crockery from the famous British-owned La Cartuja factory (now out on the Carretera de Merida). Puerta Triana (corner of Calle Santas Patronas and Calle Reyes Católicos) has a less expensive selection of painted plates, bowls and jugs while across the bridge in **Triana** Cerámica Santa Ana (Calle San Jorge 31) is a rambling showroom-cum-pottery with enough antique and modern *azulejos* to turn your home into a mini-*alcázar*. On the east side of the Maestranza bull-ring Jamón Real I – Esther Fernandez Fdez. (Calle López de Arenas 5) sells Extremaduran wines, meats and cheeses including marmalade, goats' cheese and home-made champagnes and liqueurs. It also has a small bar and there's another branch, Jamón Real II, at Calle Pastor y Landero 2.

Ceramics from Granada

Córdoba

Our word 'cordwainer' is derived from Córdoba and testifies to the city's long tradition of high quality leather-work. In the city bordering La Mezquita you'll not only find leather goods on sale in souvenir shops but also in small studios and cobblers' workshops like that at Calle Magistral González Francés 7 which specialises in riding boots. Silver filigree (*filigrana de plata*) is common, strangely a small shop in the railway station has one of the best selections. Look out also for two distinctive types of ceramic plate: the green and white Caliphal pottery based on 10th century Arab designs, and the heavy dark green pottery from nearby Lucena. Montilla wines and anis-flavoured *licor* from Rute are other specialities.

In the small shops and stalls that surround the Plaza de la Corredera you'll find tyre-soled sandals, iron rings for hanging up flower-pots, barbecue utensils and wickerwork chairs, baskets, hampers and linen chests. Near the Ayuntiamento the *guarnicionería* Rafael Estevez Lopez (Calle San Pablo 6) sells saddles, riding tackle and woollen blankets while ACA Artesanía (Calle Torres Cabrera 9) is an outlet for handicrafts made by the Asociación Cordobesa de Artesanos. This sells well-designed leather duffle bags, wallets, stationery, silverplated jewellery, toys and ceramics – much of their work is also on sale in Zoco Municipal in the Judería.

Granada

Granada's souvenirs play heavily on the city's Moorish past – embossed leather, marquetry chessboards and inlaid furniture, and a distinctive blue and green pottery known as *Fajalauza* are the most obvious examples. The Albaicín is the best place to chance upon these but you'll also find them in the Cuesta de Gomérez at the foot of Alhambra hill. Woven products from the Alpujarras mountains are worth looking at – the Tejidos Fortuny workshop (Plaza de Fortuny 1) has some lively designs of rugs and wall-hangings.

Granada's main shopping precinct lies in the streets south and east of the cathedral. Calle Pescadería has small friendly shops selling meats

Silkworms for sale in Seville's Alfalfa market

and cheeses and a stall opposite the Bar Boca has good *Fajalauza* pottery. You may find interesting bargains in the Alcaicería (the old silk-market), but elsewhere it's wall-to-wall shoeshops. If you're only here for a short stay you'd be far better off spending your money on a box of mouth-exploding cakes from Flor y Nata (Calle Mesones 51) or Lopez Mezquita (Calle Reyes Católicos 29) and heading up to the Alhambra to scoff them in the sun.

Dyed chicks in Córdoba's Corredera market

Markets

Markets are the best place to buy fresh food from the surrounding countryside. Their stalls are a cornucopia of Andalusian produce: honey, goats' cheese, spiced meats and hams, snails, seafood, olives, nuts, bread and countless glorious fruits. Markets always start early in the morning and pack up around 1pm, apart from the weekend flea markets which often linger on until 3pm.

In **Seville** every district hosts its own daily fresh produce market – one of the most central is in the Plaza de la Encarnación and another is across the Triana bridge (turn right) on the site of the old Inquisition headquarters. A small weekday arts-and-crafts market loiters outside El Corte Inglés in the Plaza del Duque de la Victoria. In the north of the city there's a centuries-old flea market on Thursday in Calle Feria known as 'El Jueves'. Nearby in the Alameda de Hércules a similar bric-a-brac market takes place on Sunday mornings. At the same time there's a charming bird and pet market (including silkworms) in the Plaza de la Alfalfa, and an earnest stamp-and-coin collector's market in the Plaza del Cabildo.

In **Córdoba** the main market venue is the Corredera. In the week there's a covered *mercado* selling fresh produce while stalls outside in the plaza sell fabric, clothes, plants and many household items of disputable necessity. On weekends this becomes a flea market.

Granada's nicest market is in the tiny Plaza Larga in the Albaicín. However you'll find a better range in and around the Mercado de San Agustín on the south-west corner of the cathedral.

Andalusian Cuisine

Seville claims to have invented *tapas* (snacks and appetizers) and can even tell you the bar where this national custom originated: El Rinconcillo (near the Santa Catalina church, Calle Gerona 40) where the staff developed the habit of covering a glass of *fino* with a *tapa* (lid) of ham. Today *tapas* are found everywhere and can be anything from a saucer of spiced olives or some slices of *jamón serrano* (mountain ham) to a gourmet nibble of oranges, onions and *bacalao* (dried cod), or a hot terracotta dish of *paella*.

A *tapa* or *porción* is simply a taster, while a *ración* is a small dish, often cooked. Lunch is the best time for *raciones* – the daily menu will be written on a board or the dishes just put out on the counter. Most bars serve *tapas* but only some treat it as an art-form. Often the bill turns out to be as costly as a meal but the repeated frisson of *fino* and *gambas* (prawns), or *cerveza* and *boquerones* (anchovies in garlic and vinegar), is quintessential Spain. If you're a serious *tapas*-addict head straight for Seville to investigate Modesto (Calle Cano y Cueto 5) or the Hostelería del Laurel (Plaza de los Venerables) in the Barrio Santa Cruz and Sol y Sombra (Calle Castilla) or Casa Manolo (Calle San Jorge) in Triana.

Most bars have an alarming array of mountain hams and spiced

Tapas bar in Seville

sausages suspended from the ceiling, all tagged like prize antiques. You could also try some *salchichón* (salami), *chorizo* (red spicy sausage) or *morcillo* (blood sausage) while *habas con jamón* (broad beans with ham) is a typical Granada dish. *Gazpacho* is another famous Andalusian creation, a chilled soup based on bread and olive oil and flavoured with vegetables and herbs – usually tomatoes, garlic and peppers. The Córdobans make their own, thicker version called *salmorejo* while *ajo blanco* is a white soup from Málaga based on garlic, almonds and fruit.

In restaurants look for regional dishes signposted with words like *andaluz, a la granadina* or *alpujarreño* (from the Alpujarras mountains). Some chefs embrace Andalusia's Moorish heritage with dishes that combine the sweet and the savoury, perhaps by using honey, fruit or raisins to spice meat and poultry. Dishes cooked in sherry or incorporating almonds are common, as are country stews (*cocido* or the simpler *puchero*) which may mix chicken, ham, sausage and egg with *garbanzos* (chick-peas), rice or potatoes.

Despite fields full of vegetables, few seem to make it onto Spanish menus. Asparagus, artichokes, aubergines (*berenjenas*) and peppers do pop up but salad is a more common complement to a main dish. There is nearly always a *revuelto* (scrambled egg dish) on the menu, perhaps mixed with salmon, mushrooms, spinach or asparagus – useful if you are vegetarian. *Tortilla sacromonte* is a Granada dish where an omelette is invaded by ham, peas and assorted offal.

Having access to both the Atlantic and Mediterranean coasts Andalusia is blessed with fresh and plentiful fish and seafood. Tuna has been a staple ingredient since pre-Roman times and sardines, swordfish (*pez espada*) and skate (*raya*) frequently feature on menus. Cuts from large fish are often served with a saffron, paprika or tomato sauce while *zarzuela* is a fish stew with a spiced tomato sauce. Fried fish can be bought in take-away *freidurías*.

Desserts always include a choice of fresh fruit or ice cream but in better quality restaurants you'll be able to dither over *tarta de almendras* (almond tart), *crema de membrillo con queso* (quince jelly with cheese), *pastel cordobés* (puff pastry with candied fruit) or the *tocino de cielo* (caramel custard) from Cádiz.

What to Eat

In cities like Seville, Córdoba and Granada people never seem to stop eating. Mornings are when work gets done and breakfast is but a meditative moment. Anything goes as long as it's quick: coffee and brandy, chocolate and *churros* (extrusions of sweet battered dough), bread dunked in olive oil, toast and dripping – all taken standing at the bar in a humble pose no doubt learned at confession. By 11am the mood shifts cakewards or to an elevenses ice-cream, but by noon the emphasis changes again as the bar staff start putting out their freshly-made *tapas*.

By 7pm it's time for the *paseo* and an obligatory ice cream, after which the *tapas* appear again around 8pm. Restaurants are in action by 9pm but rarely full before 10pm – at weekends they will still be serving new customers at midnight. After which the night is young; a good time to drink an *oloroso*, toy with a sticky cake, think what you'll have for breakfast....

Specific restaurant recommendations are included in the individual city itineraries earlier in this book. Ignore the 'fork' rating system and don't expect price to be a guarantee of quality – remem-

Heavenly sweets (see opposite)

BARRETAS
Dulce típico del
"Corpus" granadino

ber too that it is quite acceptable to just order a starter or one course if that's all you want. Keep some cash in reserve as not all restaurants take credit cards. Don't ask for the *menú del día* (menu of the day) when you really mean the *especialidad del día* (speciality of the day) – the first is a basic, low price set-meal all restaurants must offer by law (usually only advertised outside by price and often quite boring), the latter is whatever's fresh and in season.

Drinks

Andalusia's most famous drink is sherry, a fortified wine from Jerez de la Frontera. We are familiar with it as an aperitif but the Spanish will drink it with a meal and whenever they can find an excuse. It is the classic complement to *tapas*.

Sherry is perfect with tapas

Fino is the most common drink – a light, dry sherry, always served chilled. *Amontillado* is mellower with a nutty flavour and an amber hue. *Oloroso* is mature, dark and rich, often drunk as a dessert wine. *Palo cortado* is richer than *amontillado* but lighter than *oloroso*. You should also try *manzanilla*, a *fino* made in Sanlúcar de Barrameda on the Atlantic coast where the salty sea air gives it a distinctive tang.

Andalusian wines are few and come a poor second to their sherries. Exceptions are the excellent strong white Montilla-Moriles, produced in Córdoba (*amontillado* means 'like a Montilla'), and the sweet dessert wines made in Málaga from muscatel grapes.

Brandies are also produced around Jerez, varying from the cheap, highly addictive Soberano to the luxurious Carlos I. You may wish to suffer Andalusia's assorted firewaters too: the intrepid will discover a bewildering range of local *aguardientes*, variously flavoured with almonds, cherries, oranges, apricots and anis. Spanish measures of spirits are liberal, so take care.

The predominant beer is made by Cruzcampo – *una caña* is normally taken to mean a small glass of draught, *una cerveza* a large glass or a bottle. *Horchata* is an almond milk while *zumos* are heavenly fruit juices freshly-squeezed before your eyes – try a mix of *naranja* (orange) and *limón* (lemon). Bottled water is either *agua con gas* (with bubbles) or *sin gas*. Ice is unlikely to be from bottled water so if you want to avoid it ask for your drink *sin hielo*. Black coffee is *café solo*, white *con leche* and *cortado* somewhere in between. And cheers is *salud*!

Heavenly Sweets

Sweets, pastries, cakes and biscuits have been made in Andalusia's convents since the Reconquest, a sweet-toothed tradition inherited from the Arabs. Today they can still be bought from the nuns themselves. The recipe for *yemas* is centuries old, originally made from the surplus egg yolks donated to the convents after the whites had been used to clarify the wines of Jerez and Montilla. Those sold in Seville's San Leandro convent are the most famous (see Itinerary 3) but every convent makes its own delicacies.

Biscuits flavoured with honey, cinnamon, sesame, ginger or almonds are less sugary – try some *alfajores* or *polvorones* from the Convento de Santa Isabel de los Angeles in Córdoba (near the Palacio de Viana; 9–10.45am, 5–7.30pm). For a comprehensive selection of sweets from Seville's many convent-confectioneries visit El Torno (see Itinerary 2).

Bullfights

Bullfights (*corridas*) are frequently shown on Spanish television, and for many people that's quite enough. If you're keen to attend in person Seville's La Maestranza is one of the top rings in Spain. Córdoba boasts Las Califas, one of the largest *plaza de toros* in the country (on the western edge of the city) and there's also a bull-ring in Granada off the Avenida de Madrid (tickets sold at Calle Escudo del Carmen 18).

In Andalusia the bullfighting season opens with the daily *corridas* held at Seville's Feria, often some of the best fights of the year. *Corridas* continue in the city throughout May, held every Sunday at 6 or 7pm. By then the major stars will be appearing at the May Fairs held in Córdoba, Jerez de la Frontera (where the bulls are still fought on horseback), Ecija, Granada and numerous other towns. Through the summer months *corridas* only take place as a part of a local fiesta with the regular programme resumed during September and October. Posters advertising the fights are widely displayed.

Tickets for the top *corridas* can be expensive and hard to get. If you're prepared to pay for a quality spectacle it will be more apparent why bullfighting is considered an art rather than a sport. The best place to buy tickets is direct from the *Despacho Oficial de Localidades* at the *plaza de toros* but you'll also find that kiosks appear in city-centre doorways on the day before a *corrida*. These may charge a commission. Seats in the shade (*sombra*) are more expensive than those in the sun (*sol*), and you normally pay more to be near the ringside (*barrera*). Fights that include young bulls (*novillos*) usually take place at the end of the season and are cheaper.

A *corrida* is a series of six fights in which three matadors each dispatch two bulls. Each fight is a three-act drama accompanied by the tragicomic comments of a brass band. First the *bravo toro* enters and is teased and assessed by the matador and his *cuadrilla* (team); the matador then confronts the bull alone, using his cape to mock and enrage the beast. Next a *picador* enters mounted on horseback

74

inment

(it is only in this century that the horses were given protective padding), who uses a lance to damage the bull's neck muscles. The acrobatic _bandilleras_ follow, who drive colourful darts into this wound. Next the matador takes his red cloth and leads the weakened animal in a merry dance of death with slow, deft passes that reveal the extent of his courage and skill. Finally the matador thrusts his sword into the bull's heart – if it is a clean death and the matador has performed with exceptional style handkerchiefs will be waved by the crowd and, in outstanding cases, the matador will be awarded one or even two of the bull's ears.

Flamenco

Flamenco's origins are mysterious – quite appropriate for a dance form that demands spontaneity, deep emotion and an elusive, quasi-demonic power to enchant known as _duende_. Elements of ancient Indian, Arab and Jewish music have been detected in its sorrowful and discordant songs and dances, although the present guitar-backed form only evolved in the mid-18th century. Flamenco was the creation of Andalusia's gypsy communities, particularly those who settled in the Atlantic-facing lands between Seville and Cádiz. As these _gitanos_ sought work throughout Spain new local styles developed: by the late 19th century flamenco had shed its peasant image and become a public property with its own established rules and repertoire.

Flamenco's origins are mysterious

Today flamenco is crossing over into jazz and rock, and still evolving. For many it is the essence of Spain, the soul of Andalusia; for others it is just a painful caterwauling. Because it is by nature impulsive and improvised flamenco cannot lend itself to repeated public performance. Every city has its flamenco tourist shows, variously described as *tablaos* or *zambras*, which attract the vitriol of purists. They perform the fast, light-hearted *cante chico* rather than the slow, knife-in-the-heart *cante jondo*. That said, don't be put off attending a *tablao* because it's not the real McCoy. Most hotels sell tickets, inclusive of transport and a drink.

In **Seville** try Los Gallos (Plaza Santa Cruz 11) in the Barrio Santa Cruz – probably the oldest and most successful *tablao* in Andalusia, or the less tourist-wooing Tablao de Curro Vélez (Calle Rodó 7) near the bullring. In **Granada** head for the gypsy caves of Sacromonte. Unfortunately the locals seem to send out their creepiest guys to tout for business which can be off-putting – Cuevas del Rocío (Camino del Sacromonte) is the best of a mixed bunch.

For 'authentic' flamenco (which to the uninitiated may not appear all that different), music festivals, flamenco competitions and the performances staged at fiestas and fairs offer good opportunities. Seville's Feria, Córdoba's triennial Flamenco Festival and Granada's International Music and Dance Festival are three of the best (see *Calendar of Special Events*). Such occasions are natural venues for the flamenco artist to transport his or her audience.

Typical tablao in action

Nightlife

For many Spaniards this means *paseo* and *tapeo*. Promenading by the river in the evening sun or taking a gossipy walk down a central shopping street – followed by some serious *tapas* bar-hopping and/or a meal in a restaurant – is quite enough for a good night out. For wilder action in **Seville** head for the Barrio Santa Cruz or Triana (the streets west of Calle Betis); the free 'what's on' magazine *El Giraldillo* has up-to-date listings. Discotheques tend to dance in waves with teenagers arriving around 11pm and an older

Cheers from the local brewery

clientele following on about 1am: the enormous RRRrio (Calle Betis, closed Monday) caters for young lunatics and El Coto below the Hotel Los Lebreros (Calle Luis de Morales 2) for older ones. In **Granada** the streets around the University (Calle Pedro Antonio de Alarcón) set the party pace which in term-time can spread to the Sacromonte caves. For discos try the large Granada 10 (Calle Cárcel Baja 38) or Queen's Disco (Calle Arabial); Perkusion (Plaza de García) attracts teenagers and El Cadí in the Hotel Luz (Avenida de la Constitución 18) an older crowd.

Theatres and Concert Halls

Seville
Teatro de la Maestranza, *Paseo Colón. Tel: 422 28 70.*
Teatro Lope de Vega, *Avenida María Luisa. Tel: 423 45 46.*
Córdoba
Gran Teatro, *Avenida Gran Capitán. Tel: 48 02 37.*
Granada
Teatro Isabel la Catolica, *Acera del Darro. Tel: 22 32 69.*
Teatro Estable de la Universidad de Granada, *Santa Barbara 18. Tel: 28 41 43.*
Teatro Estable Corral de Comedias, *Avenida Gran Capitán 16. Tel: 20 27 25.*
Auditorio Manuel de Falla, *Paseo de los Mártires. Tel: 22 82 88.*

Sport

Seville has two **football** teams, both currently in the First Division: Sevilla (Estadio Sánchez Pizjuán in the east of the city) and Real Betis (Estadio Benito Villamarín in the south). Matches are normally played at 5pm on Sunday – any local paper (or any young Sevillian) should be able to tell you when the next fixture is.

The best **golf** courses are on the Costa del Sol but near Seville is the Pineda (members and guests only; Tel: 461 33 99) and Las Minas (Tel: 475 05 71) – both 9 holes. In Córdoba Los Villares (Tel: 35 02 08) has 18 holes, as does Granada's Los Cosarios (Tel: 26 46 53). For **skiing** contact the Sierra Nevada Ski Resort (reservations Tel: 24 91 11; weather information Tel: 48 01 53). For **hiking**, **riding**, **mountain biking**, **hang-gliding** and other adventurous pursuits in the Sierra Nevada and Alpujarras contact Global Turismo Alternativo, Tel: 76 30 54.

Calendar of Special Events

The Andalusians joke that every day, somewhere in the region, there's a fiesta going on. When you add in the boisterous stream of cultural events that major cities like Seville, Córdoba and Granada stage through the year it is inevitable that your visit will coincide with some religious holiday, local fair or arts festival.

The most spectacular and engrossing events take place between March and June. Seville's famous, histrionic **Semana Santa** (Holy Week) processions top the bill followed closely by the city's extravagant **Feria** (April Fair). Both celebrations attract large numbers of people and accommodation consequently becomes scarce and expensive – book well ahead. In May, Córdoba's **Patio Festival** and **Feria** continue the party mood while Granada's main celebrations take place around **Corpus Christi**.

To find out what's on look out for the colourful posters that warn of approaching fiestas or ask in a hotel or Tourist Office. The following calendar is only a guide and you should check dates before setting out – in Spain everything is a moveable fiesta.

JANUARY

The old year is normally seen off with a cacophony of fireworks and car horns. Tradition says you should swallow a grape (and a sip of *cava* if you're quick) for each strike of the midnight clock. Needless to say **Año Nuevo** (New Year's Day) is a public holiday.

On the second Granada celebrates the victory of the Catholic Monarchs over the city's Moorish rulers in 1492 with the **Día de la Toma** (Day of the

Poster for the spring fiestas

Capture). Regal treasures bequeathed by Ferdinand and Isabella are carried through the city and commemorative events held in the Cathedral and Capilla Real.

On the fifth the **Cabalgata del los Reyes Magos** (Calvacade of the Three Kings) celebrates their arrival with a colourful procession. The following day (the sixth) is a public holiday marking **Epiphany** (Twelfth Night), the day when Spanish children finally get their Christmas presents.

FEBRUARY

On the first Granada holds a local fiesta in honour of its patron saint **San Cecilio**, including a pilgrimage to the Sacromonte catacombs. At the end of the month, **Andalusia Day** (27 –28th) is a public holiday and celebration throughout the region.

Since the death of Franco, February in Spain has also meant **Carnaval**, an exuberant excuse for spectacular floats, fireworks, dancing and irreverence to spread to towns and villages throughout the land.

During February or March Seville stages its annual **Festival of Ancient Music** featuring early works played on authentic instruments.

MARCH/APRIL

Semana Santa (Holy Week) is a serious religious celebration with everything closed on Holy Thursday and Good Friday. Holy Week inspires the most fervent religious celebrations in the Andalusian calendar. Those held in Seville are renowned for the intense dramatic spectacle they create, but you'll find Semana Santa observed with similar panache in Málaga and with equal solemnity in Córdoba and Granada.

Events commence on Palm Sunday

when religious and social organisations known as *cofradías* (brotherhoods) start carrying revered statues and images from their chapels towards the city cathedral. Enormous ornately-decorated floats known as *pasos* are used to transport these figureheads. These precious, cumbersome platforms are steered through the narrow streets, urged on by drum bands and lamenting crowds with individuals bursting into *saetas* – brief, anguished hymns. Behind the *pasos* march columns of *nazarenos*, penitents wearing conical hoods and carrying long lighted candles.

In Seville over 100 such processions take place in the course of the week. In order to witness the greatest of these emotional tableaux – for ex-

Feria procession

ample those involving El Gran Poder, La Esperanza de Triana and La Macarena which pass through the city in the early hours of Good Friday – consult timetables and official routes published in daily newspapers like ABC, or seek the advice of a Sevillian.

Surprisingly Granada also stages an **International Tango Festival** in the first week of March. The 19th is **San José** (St Joseph's Day), a public holiday.

In mid-April Seville ignites again with its **Feria** (April Fair), a week-long fiesta of drinking, dancing and bullfighting with horse parades and Andalusian pageantry. The Feria de Abril began in the 1850s as a horse fair and agricultural market but has grown to become the best-known secular party in Andalusia.

Every spring a vast area of the Los Remedios district is transformed into a gaudy kaleidoscope of fairground attractions bordered by rows of striped drinking tents known as *casetas*. A week of sophisticated hedonism ensues with most participants dressed for the occasion – *señoritas* in bright flamenco costume cling to horsemen in wide-brimmed hats, Sevillian ladies bedecked with flowers and mantillas parade in carriages.

The day begins at noon with parades and itinerant exhibitionism, followed by bullfights at La Maestranza in the early evening. At night there is the fairground and flamenco, more *fino* and *tapas*, and ceaseless conversation. It is one of Spain's great exuberant festivals, a potent mix of corporate hospitality and gypsy singers, of banquets given by wealthy Sevillian families and shindigs hosted by political parties and trade unions. It is said that as much sherry is drunk in Feria week as is normally consumed in Spain during a year.

MAY/JUNE

On the first the **Día del Trabajo** (Labour Day) is suitably marked by a day off work. The opening days of the month are also when the *Cruces de Mayo* (Crosses of May) appear in many towns, crosses elaborately decorated with flowers that are set up in the street to herald the arrival of spring. They are best seen in Granada (especially in the Albaicín) or in Cór-

doba, and form the focus for a fiesta usually held on the third. This first week is normally when the sherry capital Jerez de la Frontera holds its annual **Feria**.

After the extravagances of Seville, May is the month when Córdoba comes alive – beginning with its charming **Festival de los Patios** (Patio Festival) usually held in the first fortnight. This is when the Córdobans open up their flower-filled courtyards to all-comers, with concerts and flamenco performances held in the neighbouring plazas. The city's festive mood culminates in the May **Feria**, held at the end of the month, when the streets are graced by elegant horseriders in Andalusian costume and the parks packed with stalls and marquees. Every three years the city also finds the energy to stage a **National Flamenco Competition**.

Not to be outdone Granada holds an **International Drama Festival** in early May while Seville stages a cultural programme of fringe theatre, dance, exhibitions and music known as '**Cita en Sevilla**' (April–June). On the 30th there is a local fiesta in Seville in honour of San Fernando. At Pentecost (Whitsun) at least half a million pilgrims descend on **El Rocío**, an isolated village to the north of Las Marismas, the marshland that lies at the mouth of the Guadalquivir river. It is the biggest *romería* (country festival) in Spain.

Corpus Christi (late May or early June) is another important Catholic celebration and public holiday honoured throughout Spain. In Seville and Córdoba choirboys in medieval dress known as Los Seises perform set dances before the Cathedral altar, while in Granada the occasion inspires the city's principal fiesta with processions, bullfights, flamenco competitions and a fair.

Cruces de Mayo celebration

Performance art festival poster

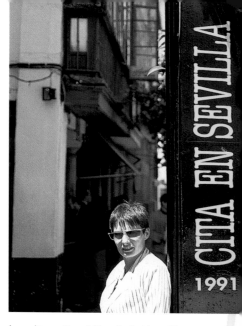

JUNE/JULY

From mid-June to mid-July Granada stages its acclaimed **International Festival of Music and Dance** which attracts top stars from the world of classical music, jazz and ballet. Some concerts take place in Charles V's palace and the patios of the Alhambra, with dance performances in the gardens of the Generalife. Córdoba holds a prestigious **International Guitar Festival** at a similar time with classical, flamenco and Latin music. On the outskirts of Seville an **International Festival of Theatre and Dance** takes place at Itálica, with performances of ballet and contemporary dance in its Roman ampitheatre.

The 25th is a public holiday, **Santiago Apóstol** (St James's Day), in honour of Spain's patron saint.

AUGUST

On the 15th there is a public holiday for **Asunción** (Assumption), and in Seville a local fiesta, the **Feast of the Virgin Kings**. During the last week the Río Guadalquivir is honoured with a festival in the sherry town of Sanlúcar de Barrameda – events include flamenco competitions and horse-racing along the beach.

SEPTEMBER

The first two weeks of September finds Ronda holding its **Feria** and *corrida goyesca*, a fight staged in 18th century costume in honour of Pedro Romero. On the eighth Córdoba celebrates its patron saint, the **Virgen de la Fuensanta**. On the last Sunday there is a fiesta in Granada in honour of the city's patroness **Nuestra Señora las Angustias**, while on the 29th in the Albaicín **San Miguel** is honoured with a fiesta and procession up to the hermitage San Miguel el Alto. Every two years Seville stages a **Festival of Flamenco** at the end of this month.

OCTOBER

Columbus's discovery of America is celebrated on the 12th with a public holiday, **Día de la Hispanidad**. There is also a local fiesta on the 24th in Córdoba in honour of **San Rafael**.

NOVEMBER

On the first, **Todos los Santos** (All Saints' Day) is a public holiday. Both Seville and Granada stage **International Jazz Festivals** this month.

DECEMBER

Constitution Day on the sixth is a public holiday, followed closely by another on the eighth, **Inmaculada Concepción**. **Navidad** (Christmas) is a traditional time for parties. Watch out for the 28th too, when Spaniards celebrate their equivalent of April Fool's Day, **Día de los Inocentes** (Day of the Holy Innocents).

PRACTICAL Information

Granada, with the advantage of being 2,247ft (685m) above sea level, is cooler and the Alhambra consequently one of the most delightful places you could spend a Spanish summer.

When to Go

Spring is the best time to visit Andalusia: any week from early March, when the orange trees are coming into blossom, to late May, when the fields and roadsides are awash with colourful wildflowers. This is the fiesta season too, when every town and village decorates its streets with flowers and coloured lights.

Accommodation for Seville's Semana Santa sells out a year in advance despite the fact that the price of a room is treble what it is for the rest of the year – an intensity that's likely to be sustained for most of 1992 while the city hosts Expo '92.

For a quieter break try and slip into a week either side of these festivities, or come in autumn – ideally September or October. During the summer the Guadalquivir valley roasts – Ecija, almost mid-way between Seville and Córdoba, is known as *la sartén* (the frying-pan) of Spain – but don't be put off: Andalusian cities, with their narrow streets, patios and gardens are designed for this heat.

Climate

In Seville and Córdoba winters are mild (12°C, 53°F) with the spring months serving as a delicious bridge into intensely hot summers that soar above 38°C (100°F) in June and July;

autumn is a slow cooling-off period as the baked land recovers. In Granada these transitions are more abrupt – spring and autumn are short, summers hot and dry (25°C, 77°F) and winters cold (6°C, 43°F). Rain tends to fall between March and October, often in sudden heavy downpours, but for most of the year the sun shines.

Time Difference

For most of the year Spanish time harmonises with the rest of Europe, one hour ahead of Britain. Spanish Summer Time runs from the last Sunday in March to the last Sunday in September, which means that during October the time in Britain and Spain is the same.

Documents

All visitors require a valid passport or a national identity card (if a citizen of an EC country). Motorists will need an international driving permit (available from international motoring organisations) or EC format three-part driving licence. If you take your own car you will need a Green Card and Bail Bond.

Money Matters

Traveller's cheques, Eurocheques and credit cards are all accepted, though far from universally. Many hotels will not accept personal cheques and not all restaurants or shops take credit cards; a cashpoint card is useful. Get some pesetas before you go.

Health

No vaccinations are required but health insurance is recommended. Form E111 entitles EC nationals to reciprocal medical benefits. A strong sun cream is essential.

Clothing

Seville, Córdoba and Granada are all smart, fashionable cities and their citizens enjoy wearing good clothes. In the summer you'll need sunglasses, sun-hat and swimming costume, but also something warm for the evenings and air-conditioned buildings; in winter a jumper and anorak will be necessary. Wear comfortable shoes at all times. A money-belt is a good idea.

Electricity

220 Volts. Sockets take round two-point plugs (European size). Most UK appliances will need an adaptor.

Photography

Film is relatively expensive in Spain and some types not always available – develop it when you get home. Carry spare camera batteries.

On Departure

In recent years Spain has had its share of air traffic delays so always confirm your return flight. When checking in be aware that there are often 'smoking' and 'no smoking' queues.

GETTING THERE

By Air

Iberia operates scheduled flights from London to Seville, Jerez de la Frontera, Málaga and Granada – some flights involve a stop-over at Madrid or Barcelona, Tel: 071-437 5622 in the UK. Other scheduled carriers operate into Málaga and Gibraltar. Charter companies also offer flight-only deals to Málaga, Gibraltar and Faro in the Portuguese Algarve – look in the classified section of local and national newspapers.

Seville airport (San Pablo) is 7.5 miles (12km) east of the city centre. A new terminal has been built as part of the preparations for Expo '92, trebling the previous capacity. There is a regular bus connection (30–40 minute trip) into the city. For Airport Information Tel: 451 06 77; for Iberia Information Tel: 422 19 02.

Granada airport is primarily used for domestic flights although there are plans to expand it. For Airport Information Tel: 44 70 81; for Iberia Information Tel: 22 75 92.

Package Deals

Travel companies offer tailor-made holidays visiting Seville, Córdoba and Granada. These include flight, accommodation and car hire. Seville is featured by city-break specialists.

By Rail

National rail networks offer through-fare deals to Andalusia (for British Rail, Tel: 071-834 2345). A new high speed rail link has reduced the journey-time between Madrid and Seville to 2¾ hours. If you are travelling extensively consider buying an Inter-Rail card or the Spanish Tarjeta Turística (available in the UK through Thomas Cook, Tel: 081-889 7777). Rail travellers can also tour Andalusia in 1920s style on the luxury Al-Andalus Express (UK contact Marsans Travel, Tel: 071-224 0504).

By Road

Coach operators offer services to Spain by road to Seville, details from Eurolines (UK Tel: 071-233 5727). If you plan to take your own car consider using the French Motorail link between Boulogne and Biarritz (contact France Ticket Service in London, Tel: 081-750 4262) or sailing from Plymouth to Santander with Brittany Ferries, Tel: 0752 221321.

GETTING AROUND

Seville is ideal for a short break and the best place in Andalusia for street-life, shopping and *tapas* bar-hopping. Córdoba is easily reached from Seville by rail or road and the two cities form a natural pair. Granada and the snow-capped Sierra Nevada are a refreshing contrast to the hot plains of the Guadalquivir valley.

Maps and Guides

If you are touring by car, Michelin map No 446 *Andalusia and the Costa del Sol* is ideal. David Baird's *Excursions in Southern Spain* (Lookout) contains 40 drives around Andalusia including detailed itineraries connecting Seville, Córdoba and Granada.

By Car

Drive on the right. Seat belts are compulsory outside built-up areas and motoring offences earn on-the-spot fines. In rural areas petrol stations may close on Sundays or for a siesta; most, but not all, take credit cards.

If you take back roads in the countryside you'll have a longer journey but a far more rewarding trip. In the cities you'll just have to take a road that isn't blocked or dug up. The Spanish treat inner-city driving as if it was a motorised bullfight, which means they see it as an art-form and therefore something to be enjoyed.

Car Hire

Many airlines and package companies offer fly-drive deals – if you know your requirements it's simplest to book before you go. It's also easy to hire cars in Spain, although some firms will not rent to drivers under 21 or with less than a year's experience. Take your passport and international driving licence – it is wise to pay a little extra for Collision Damage Waiver and Personal Accident insurance in addition to the statutory Third Party insurance. Motorbikes and mopeds can also be rented – the age limits are 18 and 16 respectively.

By Train

There are frequent trains between Seville and Córdoba (80–120 minutes). Connections from either of these cities to Granada or Málaga (3–5 hours) go via the notorious Bobadilla Junction and normally involve a change of train. The journey up from Málaga to Bobadilla is spectacular.

The Spanish have an alarming number of train classifications. Speediest are the sleek *Talgos* (supplements and reservation required), followed by the *Expresos* and *Rápidos* (both quite straightforward trains); then there are the lazy *Directos* and *Interurbanos*, followed by the utterly slothful *Tranvías*. For a free timetable ask for an *horario de trenes* – No 35 covers all connections between Seville, Córdoba, Granada and Málaga.

RENFE **Information:**
Seville Tel: 441 41 11
Córdoba Tel: 47 87 21
Granada Tel: 27 12 12

By Coach and Bus

Between Seville and Córdoba there's little to choose between train or coach but for the longer journey to or from Granada the coach is more direct and arguably more scenic. Always take a coach if you are travelling between Málaga and Granada. The most useful company is Alsina Graells who operate an hourly express service between Seville and Córdoba as well as other routes from these cities to Granada and Málaga. Tel: Seville 441 88 11; Córdoba 23 64 74; Granada 25 13 58.

A bus is a *guagua* and a stop a *parada*. If you are doing a lot of trips buy a *bonobus* 10-journey ticket from a tobacconists. For information in Seville phone 463 06 81. To visit the Itálica ruins take a bus to Santiponce.

In Córdoba the main bus station is at Avenida de Medina Azahara 29. A daily bus service to the Medina Azahara ruins leaves at 10am and returns at 12pm, although the company is very reluctant to let anyone know about this. In Granada the main station is in the Camino de Ronda.

By Taxi

Taxis are a cheap, reliable and readily available way of getting around these three cities. A green *libre* sign indicates that a taxi is for hire. Agree a price first for long journeys or tours.

Taxi Numbers
Seville Tel: 458 00 00/462 22 22.
Córdoba Tel: 47 02 91/47 51 53.
Granada Tel: 15 14 61/28 06 54.

ACCOMMODATION

Hotels

The best hotels fill up quickly. If you're taking a short break you may prefer to book an all-inclusive flight and accommodation package before you leave, plus car hire if you require it. If you are touring, ring ahead to book a room – the hotel will probably ask you to arrive by a certain time, so ring again to let them know if you will be late. Some hotels, such as the Paradors or those close to the Alhambra, are best booked as soon as you know the required dates. Hotels range from 1–5 star. Approximate prices for a double room with bath are:

☆☆☆☆☆	20,000–30,000 pesetas
☆☆☆☆	15,000–25,000 pesetas
☆☆☆	10,000–20,000 pesetas
☆☆	5,000–10,000 pesetas
☆	5,000–8,000 pesetas

IVA (Spanish VAT) of 12 per cent is added to 5 star hotels, 6 per cent to others. You may also encounter Hotel Residencias (HR) which only serve breakfast and Apartment Hotels where

rooms have kitchen facilities. *Hostales*, graded 1–3 star, are small family-run hotels offering simple accommodation that varies from the brilliant to the dismal – always see the room before you accept. Other variations are the *Pensión* (P), *Fonda* (F) and *Casas de Huéspedes* (CH). Self-catering apartments (*apartamentos turisticos*) are best booked through an agent. The minimum stay is normally a week.

A detailed list of hotels in each of these cities is available from the Spanish Tourist Office in London. Paradors (state-run luxury hotels) can be booked in the UK through Keytel International, Tel: 071-402 8182.

Seville

At present there is no Parador in Seville, although one is due to open in the monastery of San Isidoro del Campo near Santiponce for Expo '92. The nearest is in Carmona, the **PARADOR DE TURISMO ALCAZAR DEL REY DON PEDRO**☆☆☆☆, Tel: 414 10 10. Other luxury hotels include: the grand 1920s **ALFONSO XIII**☆☆☆☆☆ (Calle San Fernando 2, Tel: 422 28 50), the **DOÑA MARIA**☆☆☆☆ (in Calle Don Remondo 19, Tel: 422 49 90) and the **HOTEL MACARENA**☆☆☆☆ (Calle San Juan de Riviera 2, Tel: 437 57 00).

Alfonso XIII hotel, Seville

Pension in Córdoba

Both the **HOTEL LA RABIDA**☆☆ (Calle Castelar 24, Tel: 422 09 60) and the **HOTEL SIMON**☆ (Calle García de Vinuesa, Tel: 422 66 00) are old patio-style hotels near to the bull-ring while the pleasant **HOTEL MURILLO**☆☆ (Calle Lope de Rueda 7, Tel: 421 60 05) is in the Barrio Santa Cruz.

Córdoba

The modern **PARADOR NACIONAL LA ARRAZUFA**☆☆☆☆ stands aloof on the edge of town (Avenida de La Arrazufa 33, Tel: 27 59 00). Around the Mezquita the **HOTEL ADARVE**☆☆☆☆ (Calle Magistral González Francés 15, Tel: 48 11 02) and the **HOTEL MAIMONIDES**☆☆☆ (Calle Torrijos 4, Tel: 47 15 00) top the bill while the **HOTEL ALBUCASIS**☆☆ (Calle Buen Pastor 11, Tel: 47 86 25) and **HOTEL MARISA**☆☆ (Calle Cardenal Herrero 6, Tel: 47 31 42) are good alternatives. The **HOSTAL MAESTRE**☆☆ (Calle Romero Barros 16, Tel: 47 53 95) and the **PENSION SÉNECA** (Calle Conde y Luque 7, Tel: 47 32 34) are small, friendly family affairs with typical patios.

Granada

The **PARADOR NACIONAL SAN FRANCISCO**☆☆☆☆ (Alhambra, Tel: 22 14 40) inhabits a restored convent within the palace grounds – highly desirable but ring them now. The small **HOSTAL AMÉRICA**☆ (closed November–February; Calle Real de la Alhambra 53, Tel: 22 74 71) enjoys this privileged location too. Also on the Alhambra hill are the splendid neo-Moorish HO-

TEL **ALHAMBRA PALACE**✩✩✩✩ (Calle Peña Partida 2, Tel: 22 14 68), the modern **HOTEL LOS ALIXARES**✩✩✩ (Avenida Alixares del Generalife, Tel: 22 55 06), the old-style **HOTEL WASHINGTON IRVING**✩✩✩ (Paseo del Generalife 2, Tel: 22 75 50) and the good-value **PENSION DOÑA LUPE**✩ (Avenida de los Alixares, Tel: 22 14 73).

Down in the city centre the modern **HOTEL MELIA GRANADA**✩✩✩✩ is well-located on Calle Angel Ganivet 7 (Tel: 22 74 00), while the small **HOTEL KENIA**✩✩✩ (Calle Molinos 65, Tel: 22 75 07 and large **HOTEL LOS ANGELES** (Cuesta Escoriaza 17, Tel: 22 14 24) are south of Campo del Príncipe.

Camping

Seville: Camping Sevilla, Carretera N-IV Madrid-Cádiz km534, Tel: 51 43 79. 4 miles (6.4km) from city centre, open all year.
Córdoba: Campamento Municipal, Avenida de Brillante 50, Tel: 47 20 00. 3 miles (1.8km) from city centre, open all year.
Granada: Camping Sierra Nevada, Avenida de Madrid 107, Tel: 27 09 56. Open 15 March–15 October.

USEFUL INFORMATION

Tourist Offices

Tourist offices in Spain are generally helpful but always busy – have a list of questions ready. All can give you free maps and information and those run by the Junta de Andalusia (listed first below) also have leaflets. Every large city has a Municipal Tourist Office as well (listed second) which primarily dispenses local information. Offices are normally open 9 or 10am–1pm, 4–7 pm, including Saturday morning.
Seville Av de la Constitución 21. Tel: 422 14 04. Costurero de la Reina, Paseo de la Delicias. Tel: 423 44 65.

Córdoba Calle Torrijos 10 (Palacio de Congresos). Tel: 47 12 35. Plaza de Judá Leví. Tel: 47 20 00 ext 209.
Granada Plaza Mariana Pineda 10. Tel: 22 66 88. Calle Libreros 2. Tel: 22 59 90.

In **London** the Spanish National Tourist Office is at 57–58 St James Street, London SW1A 1LD. Tel: 071-499 0901.

Tipping and Service

Tipping is normal but not obligatory – 10 per cent for taxi-drivers and restaurants, at least 50 pesetas for hotel staff and waiters. Some restaurants will add a service charge but many people still leave a tip. In bars it costs more if you sit down at a table and are served by a waiter.

Facilities for the Disabled

Andalusia is a viable destination for disabled travellers, but facilities vary considerably. The best are found in the resorts of the Costa del Sol, although the **HOTEL INGLATERRA**✩✩✩✩ in Seville (Tel: 422 49 70) is listed as having facilities for disabled guests. For more information consult a detailed guide such as the Royal Association for Disability and Rehabilitation's annual handbook *Holidays and Travel Abroad* available in libraries or from RADAR, 25 Mortimer St, London W1. Tel: 071-637 5400.

Children

The Spanish think that children should be seen, heard and utterly spoilt. They're not just tolerated but enjoyed, welcome guests in bars and restaurants. Most hotels can provide cots and highchairs (book ahead) while baby food, nappies, powdered milk and other necessities are available in supermarkets. Babysitters can be arranged through hotels or ask Tourist Offices about private services. The larger hire car firms can supply child seats but order well in advance and take a sun-screen for the windows. It is against the law for children under 12 to travel in front seats. On RENFE children under three travel free, under seven half-price.

Duty Free

Allowances are for goods brought back to the UK having been purchased in Spanish shops (Duty Paid). If you buy goods in the airport Duty Free shop or on board a ship or plane the allowances in brackets will apply. Tobacco and alcohol allowances are only for travellers aged 17 and over.

Tobacco: 300 (200) cigarettes or 150 (100) cigarillos or 75 (50) cigars or 400g (250gms) tobacco.

Alcohol: over 38.8 proof 1.5 litres (1 litre) or not over 38.8 proof 3 litres (2 litres) or fortified/sparkling wine 3 litres (2 litres) and still table wine 5 litres (2 litres). Perfume: 75g/85.5ml (50g/57ml).

Other Goods: £250 worth (£32).

Consulates in Seville

Austria
Marqués de Paradas 26. Tel: 222162.
Britain
Plaza Nueva 8. Tel: 422 88 75.
Canada
Avenida de la Constitución 30. Tel: 229413.
France
Plaza de Santa Cruz 1. Tel: 222897.
Germany
Ramón de Carranza 22. Tel: 457811.
Netherlands
Gravina 55. Tel: 228750.
USA
Paseo de la Delicias 7. Tel: 423 18 85.

In Seville the daily newspaper *El Correo* has a general section of cultural information while *Diario 16* publishes a free 'what's on' listings magazine called *Sevilla* on Fridays. A slim listings magazine titled *El Giraldillo* is published weekly and available free from Tourist Offices, museums and cultural venues. In Córdoba the daily paper *Córdoba* has a section of useful information including late-night chemists and train and bus timetables, as does *Ideal* in Granada.

Streetside newsstand

Telephone

The Spanish telephone system is good. Phone boxes marked *Telefónica Internacional* can be used to call abroad – remember to stock up with 100 peseta coins first. They also take 5, 25 and 50 peseta coins, which you should use for local calls. You can also go to multi-boothed kiosks (*cabinas*) in the city centres. Most are open from 9am–1pm and 4–8pm. Check the assistant has put the meter back to zero before dialling.

Main Telephone Offices:
Seville: Plaza Nueva 3.
Córdoba: Plaza de las Tendillas.
Granada: Calle Reyes Católicos.

To call overseas dial 07 for an international line and wait for a high-pitched whine. Then dial the relevant country code (44 for the UK) and your number (omit the '0', eg for London dial 71 or 81). An engaged tone sounds like a rapid beeping, and the operator is 003. Calls are cheaper between 10pm and 8am.

Area codes (if calling from outside Spain omit the first '9'):

Seville province 95 (plus seven digit number)

Córdoba province 957 (plus six digit number)

Granada province 958 (plus six digit number)

Málaga province 952 (plus six digit number)

BUSINESS HOURS

Spanish hours are always vulnerable to what happened the night before, but most businesses are in action by 9am. Things stop at 1 or 1.30pm – the Spanish day is traditionally divided by a long lunch and a siesta, a practice well worth observing. Business resumes again about 4.30pm (5pm in summer) and continues till 7 or 8pm. Government offices often start at 8am and work through till 3pm.

Banks are more punctual, open 9am–2pm Monday-Friday, 9am–1pm Saturday. In summer they only open in the morning but, as in the UK, many transactions can also be done at *cajas de ahorros* (savings banks) which sometimes keep longer hours. Money can also be changed (*cambio*) at hotels and travel agents.

Post Offices (*Oficinas de Correos*) open at least 9am–1pm Monday–Saturday but avoid them if you can. Stamps (*sellos*) can be bought in tobacconists (called *estancos*, but look for a brown and yellow 'T' sign saying '*tabacos*') and most hotel receptions. A postcard within the EC costs 45 pesetas, as does a letter up to 20g.

Main Post Offices (for Poste Restante (*Lista de Correos*) mail):

Seville: Avenida de la Constitución 32. Tel: 422 88 80.

Córdoba: Calle Cruz Conde 21. Tel: 47 82 67.

Granada: Puerta Real 1. Tel: 22 48 35.

HEALTH & EMERGENCIES

Beware the sun's beguiling strength. It is very easy to get burnt, even up in the cooler mountains. Use a strong suntan cream and always drink bottled water. For minor problems chemists (*farmacias*) are a good source of advice. They are devoted solely to dispensing medication and are marked by a green cross. Don't confuse them with *droguerías* which sell perfume and toiletries. *Farmacias* have a rota of after-hours service (*farmacia de guardia*) – to find this look for a sign in the window or in the local paper. For a doctor (*médico*) or dentist (*dentista*) ask at a hotel or in the Tourist Office. State facilities are adequate – form E111 (issued by the DSS in the UK) entitles you to certain benefits, but you must first get treatment vouchers from the Instituto Nacional de la Seguridad Social (INSS), and then you can only go to doctors who operate the scheme. Good medical insurance is a better bet.

Emergencies

Police and Emergency (*urgencia*) 091.

Fire Brigade 080.

Ambulance:

Seville 433 09 93.

Córdoba 29 55 70.

Granada 22 20 24.

First Aid station (*Casa de Socorro*): **Seville** Calle Jesús del Gran Poder. Tel: 435 12 42.

Córdoba: Avenida de la República Argentina 4. Tel: 23 46 46.

Granada: Avenida de la Constitución (Main Hospital). Tel: 24 11 00.

Police

Policemen come in three colours. In urban areas the *Policía Nacional* (dark blue uniforms) rule the streets while the *Policía Municipal* (blue uniforms with a white band on their caps) control the traffic. The *Guardia Civil* (green with tricorn hats) rule everything else. Despite the sunglasses and swaggers they're all quite helpful.

Should anything happen tell your hotel or holiday representative, who should then help you inform the Policía Nacional and make a statement for insurance purposes. If you are travelling independently try to

Guardian of the streets

enlist the help of a resident to interpret. Main police stations are:

Seville: Plaza de la Gavidia. Tel: 422 88 40.

Córdoba: Avenida del Dr Fleming 2. Tel: 47 75 00.

Granada: Plaza de los Campos. Tel: 28 21 50.

Toilets

Pop into a bar, hotel or restaurant and use the *servicios* (sometimes *aseos*) – you don't have to be a customer but it is polite to ask first.

FURTHER READING

Insight Guide: Southern Spain (Apa Publications) offers up-to-date and in-depth essays on Andalusia and the Costa del Sol.

Poems of Arab Andalusia translated by Cola Franzen (City Lights Books) will transport you straight back to the enraptured world of al-Andalus. Miguel de Cervantes's *Exemplary Novels* are cautionary tales from 17th-century Spain and a good warm-up prior to tackling *Don Quixote* (both Penguin Classics). Washington Irving's *Tales of the Alhambra* is essential Granada reading (you can buy it in Granada as a cheap Everest paperback). *Here in Spain* (Lookout) by David Mitchell is an entertaining compendium of quotes from travellers in Spain over the centuries, including quips from Richard Ford's definitive 1845 guide *A Handbook for Travellers in Spain* (Centaur, 3 volumes) and George Borrow's eccentric bible-hawking autobiography *The Bible in Spain* (Century).

From this century Gerald Brenan's *South from Granada* (Cambridge) describes his life in the Alpujarras in the 1920s; Ian Gibson's *Federico García Lorca* (Faber) is a definitive biography of Spain's greatest modern poet. Alistair Boyd's *The Road to Ronda* (Collins) and Penelope Chetwode's *Two Middle-Aged Ladies in Andalusia* (Century) both describe horse-riding trips in the region made in the 1960s. Nicholas Luard's *Andalucía* (Century) and Hugh Seymour-Davies' *The Bottlebrush Tree* (Constable) both tell autobiographical tales of what it's like to set up home in a remote Andalusian village.

In the UK, all these books can be ordered through Daunt Books, 83 Marylebone High St, London W1M 4AL. Tel: 071-224 2295.

Index

A

Abd ar-Rahman I 45, 46, 47, 49
Abd ar-Rahman II 47
Abd ar-Rahman III 17, 47
al-Andalus 11, 17, 44, 45, 57
al-Hakam II 47, 48
al-Mansur 48
Almohads 12, 17, 20, 26–7, 28, 29
Almoravids 12, 17
Alpujarras 62, 68, 71, 77
Andalusia 1, 8, 9, 13, 14, 16, 17, 37, 69, 73, 76, 79, 82, 90
Andersen, Hans Christian 14
archaeology 10, 33, 63
art 13, 17, 21, 27, 31, 33, 52, 57, 65
Artespaña 65, 67
Averröes 50
'azulejos' 16, 23, 24, 29, 31, 51, 57, 59, 66, 67

B

ballet 10, 42, 43, 81
banks 89
bars 20, 26, 27, 32, 51, 52, 62, 63, 67, 70–1, 90
Berbers 11, 12, 14, 17
Bilbao, Gonzalo 33
Borrow, George 24, 90

bullfighting 9, 16, 26, 40, 50, 52, 56, 74–5, 79, 80, 81
buses 85, 88
business hours 89
Byron, Lord 27

C

Cádiz 13, 15, 71
Cano, Alonso 13, 33, 64
car hire 84, 88
'Carmen' 14, 24, 42
Carmona 10, 17, 86
carnaval 79
Carthaginians 10, 17
ceramics 22, 36, 50, 57, 66, 67, 68
Cervantes 13, 52, 90
Charles V 17, 28, 29, 46, 55–6, 57, 65
children 87–8
churches 21, 31, 32, 45, 49, 51, 53, 57, 58, 63
cinema 39, 42, 43
climate 82
coaches 84, 85
Columbus, Christopher 12, 15, 17, 20, 35, 36, 38, 81
concerts 39, 43, 43, 77, 81
consulates 88
convents 13, 25, 30, 31, 33, 51, 63, 67, 73, 86

Córdoba 9, 10, 11, 12, 13, 14, 15, 16, 17,
    22, 44–53, 68, 69, 71, 73, 74, 76, 77,
    78, 79, 80, 81, 82, 83, 84, 85, 86, 87,
    88, 89, 90
    Cathedral 48
    Judería 50–1
    La Mezquita 11, 17, 44–9
    Museo Municipal de Arte Taurino 50
    Museo Provincial de Bellas Artes 52
    Palacio de los Marqueses de Viana
        52–3
    Plaza del Potro 51–2, 53
    Puente Romano 49
    Zoco market 50, 68
Cortés 12
Costa del Sol 77, 90
Cruzcampo 38, 73

D

Dancart, Pieter 21
dance 39, 43, 79, 81
    festivals 40, 76, 81
Darro (river) 54, 57, 63
disabled, facilities for 87
discos 76–7
Disraeli, Benjamin 57
Don Juan 14, 27, 30
drama 39, 40, 42, 43, 80
    festivals 80
driving 83, 84

E

Ecija 33, 74, 82
El Córdobes 40
El Greco 33
El Rocío 80
emergencies 89
Expo '92 8, 16, 17, 19, 26, 35–43, 82,
    83, 86
    Banesto Tower 22, 39
    entertainment 39–40, 42–3
    La Cartuja 15, 36, 38, 67
    Palenque 39, 40
    Route of Discovery 37, 38, 40
    tickets 41

F

Ferdinand and Isabella 12, 15, 17, 28, 29,
    50, 57, 62, 65, 78–9
Ferdinand III 12, 17, 22, 46
'ferias' (fairs) 16, 19, 41, 74, 76, 78,
    79–80, 81
Festival de los Patios 80
fiestas 42, 76, 78–81, 82
flamenco 9, 67, 75–6, 80, 81
    festivals 76, 80, 81
Ford, Richard 14, 90
Franco, Francisco 16, 17

G

gardens 29, 30, 31, 39, 45, 58, 60, 61
Gautier, Théophile 14
Genil (river) 54
golf 77
González, Felipe 16, 17
Goya 21, 52
Granada 9, 12, 13, 14, 16, 17, 54–65,
    68–9, 71, 74, 76, 77, 78, 79, 80, 81,
    82, 83, 84, 85, 86–7, 88, 89, 90
    Albaicín 54, 62–3, 68, 69, 80, 81
    Alcaicería 65, 69
    Alcazaba 57–8
    Alhambra 12, 14, 17, 29, 54, 55–61,
        81, 82, 85, 86–7
    Capilla Real 65, 79
    Cathedral 17, 64–5, 79
    Generalife 58, 81
    Museo Arqueológico 63
    Museo Bellas Artes 57
    Museo Hispano-Musulman 56
    Nasrid palaces 56, 58, 59–61
    Sacromonte 54, 63, 76, 77, 79
Guadalquivir (river) 10, 11, 13, 16, 17,
    26, 27, 35, 40, 44, 49, 80, 81
gypsies 63, 75, 76

H, I

Hadrian 10
handicrafts 65, 66, 67, 68, 69
hang-gliding 77

Hemingway, Ernest 16
Herrera, Juan de 25
hotels 23, 37, 41, 44, 58, 85–7, 90
Iberians 10
Ibero-American Exposition 14, 17, 19, 23–4, 33, 37
Ibn-al-Ahmar 12, 57
Inquisition 12, 13
Irving, Washington 14, 57, 61, 90
Isla de la Cartuja 26, 35, 37
Itálica 10, 17, 20, 32, 33, 40, 81

J, L

Jaén 10, 12
jazz 43, 76, 81
Jerez de la Frontera 40, 73, 74, 80, 83
jewellery 10, 50, 66, 67, 68
Jews 12, 25, 50, 51
Juan Carlos I 16, 17, 35
La Pileta 17
La Rábida 15
Las Marismas 10, 80
Las Navas de Tolosa 12, 17
Leal, Valdés 13, 27, 33
leather 40, 51, 52, 61, 66, 68
Lorca, Federico García 16, 90
Lucan 10

M

Machuca, Pedro 55–6
Madrid 17, 83
Magellan 13, 38
Maimónides 50
Málaga 71, 83, 85, 89
maps 84
markets 25, 26, 32, 50, 52, 62, 64, 65, 68, 69
Medina Azahara 11, 85
Mérimée, Prosper 24
Moors 11, 12, 17, 29, 31, 44, 45, 51, 54, 57, 60, 73, 78
'moriscos' 13, 62
mountain-biking 77
mudéjar style 16, 30, 31, 33, 46, 47, 50, 51, 59, 60

Murillo 13, 21, 27, 33
museums 10, 26, 27, 33, 50, 51, 52, 56, 57, 63, 65, 88
music 39, 50, 63, 67, 76, 79, 81
festivals 76, 81

N, O

Nasrid dynasty 9, 12, 17, 55, 57, 58
newspapers 88
nightlife 75–77
opera 27, 42, 43

P

Pacheco, Francisco 33
passports 83, 84
'patios' 19, 22, 27, 28, 29, 32, 44, 45, 46, 47, 51, 80, 86
Pedro I (the Cruel) 12, 17, 19, 28, 29, 31
Peninsular War 14, 17, 36
pharmacies 88, 89
Philip II 29, 49
Phoenicians 10, 11, 17
Pickman, Charles 36
police 89, 90
population 13, 62
post offices 89
public holidays 78, 79, 80, 81

R

Reconquest 12, 22, 28, 57
restaurants 23, 32, 39, 44, 51, 52, 58, 63, 65, 72, 90
river cruises 27, 40
Rivera, Primo de 14
Romans 10, 11, 17, 33, 44, 49, 50, 52
Romero, Pedro 81
Ronda 17, 81

S

Sanlúcar de Barrameda 10, 15, 73, 81
Santiponce 10, 86
Semana Santa (Holy Week) 19, 21, 41, 42, 78, 79, 82
Seneca 10
Seville 9, 12, 13, 14, 15, 16, 17, 19–43,

67, 69, 70, 73, 74, 76, 77, 78, 79–80, 81, 82, 83, 84, 85, 86, 87, 88, 89, 90
  Archivo General de Indias (Lonja) 13, 25
  Ayuntiamento 32
  Barrio Santa Cruz 25, 30, 76
  Capilla Mayor 20
  Capilla Real 22
  Casa de la Contratación 12, 13, 28
  Casa de Pilatos 30–1
  Cathedral 17, 19, 15, 20–22, 79, 80
  Hospital de la Caridad 27
  La Cartuja 15, 36, 38, 67
  La Giralda 12, 17, 19, 20–22
  La Maestranza (bullring) 25, 26, 40, 74, 77, 80
  Murillo Gardens 30
  Museo Arqueológico 33
  Museo de Bellas Artes 33
  Museo de Artes y Costumbres Populares 33
  Parque de María Luisa 23, 24, 33
  Reales Alcázares 12, 17, 27–9, 31
  Teatro de La Maestranza 27, 40, 42, 43, 77
  Teatro Lope de Vega 40, 42, 43, 77
  Tobacco Factory 14, 17, 19, 24, 33
  Torre del Oro 12, 26
  Triana district 26, 67, 76
shoes 53, 66, 67, 68
shopping 25, 32, 50, 51, 53, 65, 66–9
Sierra Morena 12, 44
Sierra Nevada 12, 54, 63, 77, 84
silk 11, 65, 68, 69
Siloé, Diego de 64
silver 50, 66, 68
Spanish Civil War 16, 17
synagogues 51

T

'tapas' 23, 27, 32, 50, 63, 70–1, 72, 73, 76
Tarifa 11
Tartessus 10, 17, 33
taxis 85

telephones 88–9
theatres 27, 39, 40, 42, 43, 77, 80
Toledo 10, 51
Torres, Julio Romero de 52
tourism 14, 16
Tourist Offices 23, 78, 86, 87, 88, 89
trains 8, 41, 84, 85, 88
Trajan 10

U–Z

Ummayad dynasty 9, 12, 17, 45
Van Dyck 21
Velázquez 13, 33
Vespucci, Amerigo 12
Visigoths 10, 17, 22, 45, 46, 49, 50
War of the Spanish Succession 13
'yemas' 32, 73
Zurbarán 13, 21, 30, 33

Art & Photo Credits

Photography

4, 10T, 11, 12B, 13, 14, 23, 27B, 28, 29, 31B, 32T, 33, 47, 49, 53, 55, 56, 58, 62, 63, 65B, 66, 67, 70T, 72, 73, 74, 75T, 76, 78, 80, 81, 82, 86T, 87, 89 — **Nigel Tisdall**

1, 12T, 16, 21, 24, 26, 45, 48, 50, 52, 60T, 61, 70B, 71, 77, 84, 86B — **Lyle Lawson**

64, 65T — **Capilla Real**

15 — **Andrew Eames**

35, 36, 37, 38, 39T, 43 — **Expo '92**

10B, 19, 22T, 27T, 39B, 40, 60B, 68T, 75B, 79, 83, 90 — **Junta de Andalucia**

30, 31T — **St John O'Rourke**

8, 22, 32B, 42, 68B, 69 — **Alice Prier**

Publisher	**Hans Höfer**
Design Concept	**V Barl**
Designer	**Patrick Wong**
Layout	**Erich Meyer**
Cover Design	**Klaus Geisler**
Managing Editor	**Andrew Eames**
Editor	**Elizabeth Boleman-Herring**
Production Editor	**Gareth Walters**
Cartography	**Berndtson & Berndtson**

Andalusia

40 km / 25 miles

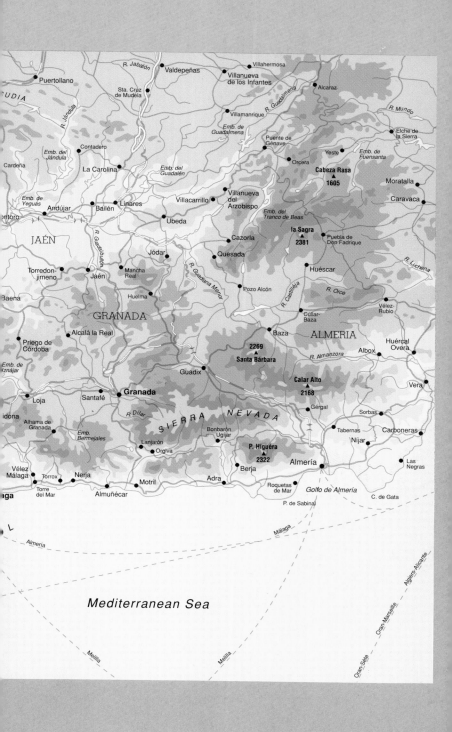